zero
limits

The Secret
Hawaiian System
for Wealth, Health,
Peace, *and* More

JOE VITALE
IHALEAKALA HEW LEN, PhD

WILEY

John Wiley & Sons, Inc.

Published by John Wiley & Sons, Inc., Hoboken, New Jersey.
Published simultaneously in Canada.

Wiley Bicentennial Logo: Richard I. Pacifico.

For general information on our other products and services or for technical support, please contact our Customer Care Department within the United States at (800) 762-2974, outside the United States at (317) 572-3993 or fax (317) 572-4002.

Wiley also publishes its books in a variety of electronic formats. Some content that appears in print may not be available in electronic books. For more information about Wiley products, visit our web site at www.wiley.com.

Library of Congress Cataloging-in-Publication Data:

Vitale, Joe, 1953–
    Zero limits : the secret Hawaiian system for wealth, health, peace, and more / Joe Vitale, Ihaleakala Hew Len.
        p.   cm.
    Includes bibliographical references (p.   ).
    ISBN 978-0-470-10147-6 (cloth)
    1. Success—Religious aspects.   I. Hew Len, Haleakala.   II. Title.
BL65.S84V58   2007
204'.4—dc22

                                                                    2007002385

Printed in the United States of America.

To Morrnah and Ka'i
—Dr. Hew Len

To Mark Ryan and Nerissa
—Dr. Vitale

Ho'oponopono is a profound gift that allows one to develop a working relationship with the Divinity within and learn to ask that in each moment, our errors in thought, word, deed, or action be cleansed. **The process is essentially about freedom, complete freedom from the past.**

—Morrnah Nalamaku Simeona,
Ho'oponopono Master Teacher,
creator of Self I-Dentity Ho'oponopono,
named a Living Treasure
of the State of Hawaii in 1983
by the Hongwanji Mission of Honolulu
and the Hawaii State Legislature

Acknowledgments

Two key people deserve thanks for this book: Mark Ryan is the priceless friend who first told me the story of the unusual therapist you're about to read about, and Dr. Ihaleakala Hew Len is that unusual therapist who has become my latest priceless friend. Nerissa, my love, is my main support person and domestic life partner. Matt Holt and my dear friends at John Wiley & Sons, Inc. are terrific people to know and work with. Suzanne Burns is my key assistant and publicist, and proofread an early draft of this manuscript. My mastermind group supported me in this project, including Jillian Coleman-Wheeler, Cindy Cashman, Craig Perrine, Pat O'Bryan, Bill Hibbler, and Nerissa Oden. Early readers of this book who helped me shape it and perfect it include Mark Weisser and Mark Ryan. I also want to thank the Divine for guiding me in the process of writing this book. I am grateful to all.

Contents

Preface

Where Peace Begins

Dear Morrnah Nalamaku Simeona, the creator and first master teacher of Self I-Dentity Ho'oponopono, had on her desk a placard that read, "Peace begins with me."

I witnessed this peace beyond all understanding as I worked and traveled with her from December 1982 to that fateful day in Kirchheim, Germany, in February 1992. Even as she lay in death on her bed surrounded by chaos, she exuded that stillness beyond all understanding.

It was my great good fortune and honor to have received the training from Morrnah in November 1982 and to have been in her presence for a decade. I have been doing Self I-Dentity Ho'oponopono ever since. I am pleased that, with the help of my friend Dr. Joe Vitale, this message can now reach the world.

But the truth is it only has to reach you, through me, as we are all one and it all happens inside.

Peace of I,
Ihaleakala Hew Len, PhD
Chairman Emeritus
The Foundation of I, Inc. Freedom of the Cosmos
www.hooponopono.org   www.businessbyyou.com

Introduction

The Secret of the Universe

In 2006 I wrote an article titled "The World's Most Unusual Therapist." It was about a psychologist who helped heal an entire ward of mentally ill criminals—without ever seeing any of them professionally. He used an unusual healing method from Hawaii. Until 2004, I had never heard of him or his method. I searched for two years before I found him. I then learned his method and wrote that now-famous article.

That article swept the Internet. It was posted on newsgroups and e-mailed to huge lists of people from all walks of life. My own list at www.mrfire.com loved it, and passed it on to tens of thousands of others. They in turn forwarded it to family and friends. I estimate about five million people saw that article.

Everyone who read it found it hard to believe. Some were inspired. Some were skeptical. All wanted more. This book is a result of their desire and my quest.

Even if you're a veteran of the five steps in my earlier book, *The Attractor Factor*, you may not understand the incredible insights I'm about to reveal to you here, at least not at first glance. The simple process I'm going to share in this book will help explain why I've been able to manifest some huge accomplishments without actually trying to make them happen. Here are a few of them:

- My Nightingale-Conant audio program, *The Power of Outrageous Marketing*, happened *after* I quit pounding on their door for 10 years.

- How did I go from homeless to poverty to struggling writer to published author to best-selling author to Internet marketing guru *with no plan at all?*

- My desire to attract a BMW Z3 sports car led to me *being inspired* with an Internet marketing idea no one had ever thought of before—which made me $22,500 in one day and a quarter of a million dollars in a year or so.

- My desire to buy and move into a Texas hill country estate when I was broke and going through a divorce led to me creating a new business that brought in $50,000 *in one day*.

- My huge weight loss of 80 pounds occurred *after* I gave up and opened myself to a new way to achieve my desire.

- My desire to be the author of a #1 best-selling book led to my writing a #1 best-selling book that I *never planned* to write at all and *wasn't even my idea*.

- My appearance in a hit movie, *The Secret*, happened without my begging, pleading, intending, or orchestrating *anything at all*.

- My appearance on *Larry King Live* in November 2006, and again in March 2007, happened without my ever intending it.

- As I write these words, Hollywood hotshots are talking about turning my book, *The Attractor Factor*, into a movie, and still others are negotiating to get me my own television program.

The list could go on, but you get the idea. I have many miracles happening in my life.

But *why* are they happening?

I was once homeless. Today I'm a best-selling author, Internet celebrity, and multimillionaire.

What happened to me to create all this success?

Yes, I followed my dreams.

Yes, I took action.

Yes, I was persistent.

Haven't a lot of other people done those same things and yet not achieved success?

What's different?

If you look at the accomplishments I've listed with a critical eye, you might see that none of them were directly created by me. In fact, what they all have in common is a spirit of Divine planning, with me a sometimes unwilling participant.

Let me explain this another way: Toward the end of 2006 I taught a seminar called Beyond Manifestation (www.Beyond Manifestation.com), which is heavily influenced by what I learned after I discovered the mysterious Hawaiian therapist and his method. In that event I asked everyone to list all the ways they knew to manifest or attract something in their life. They said things like affirmations, visualizations, intentions, body awareness methods, feeling the end result, scripting, Emotional Freedom Technique (EFT) or tapping, and many, many more. Once the group inventoried every single way they could come up with to create their own reality, I asked them if those ways worked all the time, without exception.

Everyone agreed they did not always work.

"Well, why not?" I asked them.

No one could say for sure.

I then hit the group with my observation:

"All of those ways have limitations," I declared. "They are toys your mind plays with to keep you thinking you're in charge. The truth is, you are not in charge, and the real miracles come when you let go of the toys and trust in a place inside yourself where there are zero limits."

I then told them that where you want to be in life is *behind* all of those toys, which is behind the chatter of the mind and right there with what we call the Divine. I went on to explain that there are at least three stages to life, beginning with you as victim, then moving on to you as creator of your life, and ending—if you're lucky—with you becoming servant to the Divine. In that last stage, which I'll discuss later in this book, astonishing miracles happen—almost without you trying.

Earlier today I interviewed a goals expert for my Hypnotic Gold membership program. (See www.HypnoticGold.com.) He has written a dozen books and sold millions of copies of them. He knows how to teach people how to set goals. Most of his philosophy revolves around having a burning desire to accomplish something. But that's an incomplete strategy. I asked him what he suggested when someone can't find the motivation to set a goal, let alone complete it.

"If I knew that," he began, "I'd be able to solve most of the problems in the world."

He went on to say that you have to be hungry to achieve a goal. If you aren't, you won't keep up the discipline needed to focus on it and work toward it.

"But what if you're not hungry enough?" I asked.

"Then you won't reach your goal."

"How do you make yourself hungry or motivated?"

He couldn't answer.

And that's the rub. At a certain point all the self-help and goal-setting programs fail. They come up against the troubling fact that if someone isn't ready to achieve something, they won't maintain the energy needed to manifest it. They'll quit. Everyone knows this experience from setting resolutions on January 1st and forgetting them by January 2nd. The good intentions were there. But something deeper wasn't in alignment with the conscious desires.

So how do you take care of that deeper state that isn't "hungry"?

That's where the Hawaiian method you'll learn in the book comes in handy. It helps clean the *unconscious*, which is where the block resides. It helps dissolve the hidden programs that keep you from attaining your desires, whether health, wealth, happiness, or anything else. It all happens inside you.

I'll explain all of this in the book you are holding right now. For now, consider this:

There's a quote from Tor Norretranders' book, *The User Illusion*, that sums up the essence of the mental roller-coaster ride you're about to embark on: "The universe began when nothing saw itself in the mirror."

In short, *Zero Limits* is about returning to the zero state, where nothing exists but anything is possible. In the zero state there are no thoughts, words, deeds, memories, programs, beliefs, or anything else. Just nothing.

But one day nothing saw itself in the mirror and you were born. From there, you created, and unconsciously absorbed and accepted, beliefs, programs, memories, thoughts, words, deeds, and more. Many of these programs go all the way back to the beginning of existence itself.

The whole purpose of this book is to help you to experience wonder moment by moment. From that place, miracles like the ones I described will happen to you. They'll be unique to you. And they'll be just as marvelous, magical, and miraculous.

My experience of this spiritual rocket ship into power beyond comprehension has been almost indescribable. I have success beyond my wildest dreams. I have new skills, and my level of love for myself and the world is on a level of understanding words often fail to describe. I live in a near-constant state of awe.

Let me put it this way: Everyone has a lens through which they view the world. Religions, philosophies, therapies, authors, speakers, gurus, and candlestick makers all perceive the world through a particular mind-set. What you'll learn in this book is how to use a new lens to dissolve all other lenses. And once you succeed, you'll be at the place I call zero limits.

Please understand that this is the first book in history to reveal this updated Hawaiian method for healing, called Self I-Dentity Ho'oponopono. But also please understand that this is just one man's experience with the method: mine. While this book is written with the blessing of the therapist who taught me the amazing method, everything to follow is written through my own lens of the world. To fully understand Self I-Dentity Ho'oponopono, you need to attend a weekend training and experience it for yourself. (Trainings are listed at www.hooponopono.org and www.zerolimits.info.)

Finally, the entire essence of this book can be summed up in one phrase—a phrase you will learn to use; a phrase that reveals the ultimate secret of the universe; a phrase that I want to say to you and the Divine right now:

"I love you."

Take a ticket and have a seat. The train into your soul is about to take off.

Hold on to your hat.

> I love you.
> *Aloha no wau ia oe.*
> Dr. Joe Vitale
> (Ao Akua)
> Austin, Texas
> www.mrfire.com

The universe began when nothing saw itself in the mirror.

Tor Norretranders, *The User Illusion*

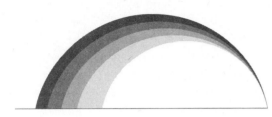

The Adventure Begins

Peace be with you, all my Peace.
O ka Maluhia no me oe, Ku'u Maluhia a pau loa.

I n August 2004, I was speaking and working a booth at the National
Guild of Hypnotists annual convention. I enjoyed the people, the
event, the energy, and the networking. But I wasn't prepared for the
life-changing event that would begin that day.

My friend Mark Ryan was working the booth with me. Mark is
a hypnotherapist, as well. He's very open-minded, curious, articulate,
and penetrating when it comes to exploring life and all its mysteries.
We often had conversations that lasted for hours. We talked about our
heroes in therapy, from Milton Erickson to lesser-known shamans. It
was during one of these conversations that Mark surprised me by
asking,

"Have you ever heard of the therapist who healed people without ever seeing them?"

The question stopped me. I had heard of psychic healers and re-
mote or distance healers, but Mark seemed to be suggesting something different.

"He's a psychologist who healed an entire mental hospital full of
the criminally insane, but he never saw a single patient."

"What did he do?"

"He used a Hawaiian healing system called ho'oponopono."

"Ho-oh-*what*?" I asked.

I asked Mark to repeat the term about a dozen times. I had never heard it before. Mark didn't know the story, or the process, well enough to tell me much more. I admit I was curious, but I also confess that I was skeptical, as well. I figured this had to be an urban legend. Heal people without seeing them? Yeah, right.

Mark went on to tell me the following story:

"I had been traveling to Mount Shasta in California for about 16 years in search of myself," Mark explained. "One friend there gave me a little booklet that I never forgot. It was white paper with blue ink. It was an article about this Hawaiian therapist and his method. I read that article over and over again for years. It didn't describe what the therapist actually did, but it said he healed people with his method."

"Where's that article now?" I asked. I wanted to read it.

"I can't find it," Mark said. "But something told me to tell you about it. I know you don't believe me, but I'm as fascinated as you are. I want to know more, too."

A year passed before the next convention. During the intervening months, I poked around online but couldn't find anything about any therapist who cured people without seeing them. Sure, there's information on distance healing, where someone heals another without the other person being present, but I understood that the Hawaiian therapist didn't do that. As I would come to learn, there's no distance *at all* in the type of healing he did. On top of all that, I didn't know how to spell *ho'oponopono* to look it up online. So I let it go.

Then, in 2005, at the next annual hypnosis convention, Mark again mentioned the therapist.

"Did you ever find anything about him?" he asked.

"I don't know his name, and I don't know how to spell ho-whatever that term is," I explained. "So I couldn't find a thing."

Mark's a go-getter. We took a break, pulled out my laptop, found a wireless Internet connection, and went searching. It didn't take long to find the main and only official site for ho'oponopono at www.hooponopono.org. I looked around and saw a few articles. They gave me a quick overview of what I was about to get into.

I found a definition of ho'oponopono: "Ho'oponopono is a process of letting go of toxic energies within you to allow the impact of **Divine** thoughts, words, deeds, and actions."

I had no idea what that meant, so I looked around some more. I found this:

"Simply put, Ho'oponopono means, 'to make right,' or 'to rectify an error.' According to the ancient Hawaiians, error arises from thoughts that are tainted by painful memories from the past. Ho'o-ponopono offers a way to release the energy of these painful thoughts, or errors, which cause imbalance and disease."

Interesting, yes. But what did it mean?

As I explored the site, looking for information on the mysterious psychologist who healed people without seeing them, I learned that there is an updated form of ho'oponopono called Self I-Dentity through Ho'oponopono (SITH).

I didn't pretend to know what all of this meant. Mark didn't pretend, either. We were fellow explorers. Our laptop was the horse we rode into the wilderness of this new land. We were in search of answers. We eagerly typed forward.

We found an article that helped explain a few things:

Self I-Dentity Through Ho'oponopono
Being 100 Percent Responsible for the Problems of
My Clients
By Ihaleakala Hew Len, PhD, and Charles Brown, LMT

In traditional approaches to problem solving and healing, the therapist begins with the belief that the source of the problem is within the client, not within him. He believes that his responsibility is to assist the client in working through his problem. Could these beliefs have re-sulted in systemic burnout throughout the healing profession?

To be an effective problem solver, *the therapist must be willing to be 100 percent responsible for having created the problem situation; that is, he must be willing to see that the source of the problem is erroneous thoughts within him, not within the client. Therapists never seem to notice that every time there is a problem, they are always present!*

Being 100 percent responsible for actualizing the problem allows the therapist to be 100 percent responsible for resolving it. Using the updated Ho'oponopono approach, a process of repentance, forgiveness, and transmutation developed by Kahuna Lapa'au Morrnah Nalamaku Simeona, a therapist is able to have erroneous thoughts within himself and within the client transmuted into perfect thoughts of LOVE.

Her eyes brim with tears. Deep trenches enclose the corners of her mouth. "I am worried about my son," Cynthia sighs softly. "He's back on drugs again." As she tells her painful story, *I begin the cleaning of the erroneous thoughts within me that have actualized as her problem.*

As erroneous thoughts are replaced by loving thoughts in the therapist and in his family, relatives, and ancestors, they are replaced too in the client and in her family, relatives, and ancestors. The updated Ho'oponopono process allows the therapist to work directly with the Original Source who can transmute erroneous thoughts into LOVE.

> Her eyes dry up. The trenches around her mouth
> soften. She smiles, relief dawning across her face.
> "I don't know why, but I'm feeling better." I do not
> know why, either. Really. Life is a mystery except to
> LOVE, who knows all. I just let it go at that, and just
> thank LOVE from whom all blessings flow.

In problem solving using the updated Ho'oponopono process, the therapist first takes his I-Dentity, his Mind, and connects it up with the Original Source, what others call LOVE or GOD. With the connection in place, the therapist then appeals to LOVE to correct the erroneous thoughts within him that are actualizing as the problem for himself first and for the client second. The appeal is a process of repentance and forgiveness on the part of the therapist—"I am sorry for the erroneous thoughts within me that have caused the problem for me and for the client; please forgive me."

In response to the repentance and forgiveness appeal of the therapist, LOVE begins the mystical process of transmuting the erroneous thoughts. In this spiritual correction process, LOVE first neutralizes the erroneous emotions that have caused the problem, be they resentment, fear, anger, blame, or confusion. In the next step, LOVE then releases the neutralized energies from the thoughts, leaving them in a state of void, of emptiness, of true freedom.

With the thoughts empty, free, LOVE then fills them with Itself. The result? The therapist is renewed, restored in LOVE. As the therapist is renewed so is the client and all involved in the problem. Where there was despair in the client, there is LOVE. Where there was darkness in her soul, there is now the healing Light of LOVE.

The Self I-Dentity through Ho'oponopono training teaches people who they are and how they can solve problems moment to moment, and in the process be renewed and restored in LOVE. The training begins with a two-hour free lecture. Attendees are given an overview of how thoughts within them actualize as spiritual, mental, emotional, physical, relational, and financial problems in their lives and in the lives of their families, relatives, ancestors, friends, neighbors, and associates. In the weekend training, students are taught what a problem is, where the problems are located, how to solve different kinds of problems using over 25 problem solving processes, and how to really take good care of themselves. The underlying emphasis in the training is on being 100 percent responsible for themselves and for what happens in their lives and for solving problems effortlessly.

The wonder of the updated Ho'oponopono process is that you get to meet yourself anew each moment, and you get to appreciate more and more with each application of the process the renewing miracle of LOVE.

> **I operate my life and my relationships according to the following insights:**
>
> 1. The physical universe is an actualization of my thoughts.
> 2. If my thoughts are cancerous, they create a cancerous physical reality.
> 3. If my thoughts are perfect, they create a physical reality brimming with LOVE.
> 4. I am 100 percent responsible for creating my physical universe the way it is.
> 5. I am 100 percent responsible for correcting the cancerous thoughts that create a diseased reality.
> 6. There is no such thing as out there. Everything exists as thoughts in my mind.

Mark and I read the article and wondered which author was the therapist we sought: Charles Brown or this Dr. Hew Len. We didn't know. We couldn't tell. And who was this Morrnah the article mentioned? And what was Self I-Dentity Ho-oh-*please*?

We read on.

We found a few more articles that shed light on what we sought. They included revealing statements, such as: "Self I-Dentity through Ho'oponopono sees each problem not as an ordeal, but as an opportunity. Problems are just replayed memories of the past showing up to give us one more chance to see with the eyes of LOVE and to act from inspiration."

I was curious but I wasn't getting it. Problems were "replayed memories of the past"? Huh? What were these authors trying to explain? How did this ho-whatever help the therapist who healed people? Who was this therapist, anyway?

I found yet another article, this one by a reporter named Darrell Sifford, who wrote about meeting the creator of this ho'opo-whatever process. Her name is Morrnah and she's a kahuna, or keeper of the secrets. What this Morrnah does to help heal people is "appeal to the divine creator of our choice 'through the divinity that is within each person . . . who is really an extension of the divine creator.'"

Maybe you understand that. I didn't at the time. Neither did Mark. Apparently this Morrnah said some words, like a prayer, that helped people heal. I made a mental note to locate that prayer, but right now I was going on a different mission: to find the therapist and learn his method for healing. My eagerness to know more and to meet this shaman therapist was becoming more and more exciting. Even though Mark and I really needed to be back at our booth at the convention, we let it slide so we could continue our quest.

Based on the articles and web site, we guessed the therapist we wanted to find was named Ihaleakala Hew Len. Some first name. I had no idea how to pronounce it, let alone spell it. I didn't know how to locate him, either. The site didn't have any contact information for him. Mark and I tried to Google him, but turned up nothing. We began to wonder if this ethereal therapist was a fiction, or retired or even deceased.

I closed my laptop and went back to the convention.

But the adventure had begun.

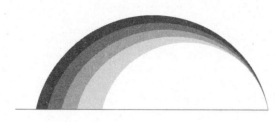

Finding the World's Most Unusual Therapist

Who looks outside, dreams; who looks inside, awakes.

—Carl Jung

B ack in my home outside of Austin, Texas, I couldn't shake the story of the therapist who cured people without seeing them. What was his method? Who was he? Was the story a hoax?

Because of my 20-some years in personal development, mostly chronicled in my books *Adventures Within* and *The Attractor Factor*, it shouldn't be a surprise to anyone that I needed to know more. I've always been curious. I spent seven years with a controversial guru. I interviewed self-help mentors and sages, authors and speakers, mystics and magicians of the mind. Because of the success of my current books, I could now call many of the leading experts in the field of human development my friends. But I couldn't shake the story of this therapist. This was different. This was a breakthrough.

I needed to know more.

So I again went searching. In the past I've hired private detectives to locate missing people. I did it when I wrote about advertising genius Bruce Barton for my book *The Seven Lost Secrets of Success*. I was ready to hire a professional to find Dr. Hew Len, too, when an odd thing happened.

One day, while doing yet another search for Dr. Hew Len, I found his name associated with a web site. I have no idea why this didn't surface before, in earlier searches. But there it was.

I couldn't find a phone number. But I could hire Dr. Hew Len for a personal consultation by e-mail. It seemed like an odd way to do therapy, but in these Internet times, anything goes. Figuring that would be the best way to get a foot in his door, I sent him an e-mail through the web site. I was excited beyond words. I could hardly wait for his reply. What would he say? Would he write something enlightening? Would he heal me by e-mail?

I could barely sleep that night, I was so eager to hear from him. By the next morning, he responded, writing:

Joe:

Thank you for requesting a consultation. Consultations are usually done via the Internet or by fax. The person requesting the consultation provides information for me about the nature of the consultation, i.e., a description of a problem, of a concern. I process and meditate on the information for Divine directions. Then I communicate back to the person via e-mail what I received in meditation.

While I was out for lunch today, a lawyer-client from Hawaii faxed me information to look at. After processing it, I will get back to him what I received from Divinity in meditation.

Information about the nature of my work can be gained at www.hooponopono.org.

Please feel free to contact me to see what will work for you.

I wish you Peace beyond all understanding.

Peace of I,

Ihaleakala Hew Len, PhD

It was an odd e-mail. He talks to Divinity? Lawyers hire him? I didn't know enough yet to pass judgment on him or his methods, but I sure wanted to know more.

I instantly decided to hire him for a consultation by e-mail. It would cost $150. To me, that was nothing. I was finally going to hear from the long-sought-after miracle-working psychologist! I was excited!

I gave some thought to what I should ask him about. I'm doing pretty well in my life. I've got the books, the successes, the cars, homes, life partner, health, and happiness most people seek. I had lost 80 pounds and was feeling great, but I also had maybe 15 pounds left to release. Since I was still struggling with weight loss issues, I decided to ask Dr. Hew Len for a consultation about that. I did. He responded within 24 hours, writing this e-mail to me:

Thank you, Joe, for your reply.

When I looked I heard, "He's fine."

Talk to your body. Say to it: "I love you the way you are. Thank you for being with me. If you have felt abused by me in any way, please forgive me." Stop now and then during the course of the day visit with your body. Let the visit be one of love and thankfulness. "Thank you for conveying me about. Thank you for breathing, for the beating of our heart."

See your body as a partner in your life, not as a servant. Talk to your body as you would talk to a little child. Be friends with it. It likes lots and lots of water to work better with its self. You may feel that it is hungry, yet it may be telling you that it is thirsty.

Drinking Blue Solar Water transmutes memories, replaying problems in the subconscious mind (the Child), and helps the body to "Let go and let God." Get a blue glass bottle. Fill it up with tap water. Cork the top of the bottle or wrap the top in cellophane. Place the bottle in the sun or under an incandescent lamp for at least one hour. Drink the water; rinse your body with the water after bathing or showering. Use the Blue Solar Water to cook with, wash your clothes with, and for whatever you use water for. You can make your coffee or hot chocolate with Blue Solar Water.

Your e-mail has the feel of elegant simpleness, a gift beyond compare.

Perhaps we can visit again as a fellow traveler clearing our way homeward.

I wish you Peace beyond all understanding.

Peace of I,

Ihaleakala

While I enjoyed the peacefulness of his message, I was left wanting more. Was this how he gave consultations? Was this how he healed those people in the mental hospital? If so, something was seriously missing. I doubt that most people would have accepted his e-mail as the final verdict on a weight loss issue. Telling me, "You're fine" isn't exactly a solution to anything.

I wrote back, asking for more information. Here's what he wrote in reply:

Joe:

Peace begins with me.

My problems are memories replaying in my subconscious. My problems have nothing to do with anyone or anyplace or any situation. They are what Shakespeare so poetically noted in one of his sonnets as "fore-bemoanèd moans."

When I experience memories replaying problems, I have choice. I can stay engaged to them or I can petition Divinity to free them up through transmutation, thus restoring my mind to its original state of zero, of void . . . of being memory free. When I am memory free, I am my Divine Self as Divinity created me in its exact likeness.

When my subconscious is in zero state, it is timeless, boundless, infinite, deathless. When memories dictate, it is stuck in time, place, problems, uncertainty, chaos, thinking, coping, and managing. In allowing memories to rule, I give up clarity of mind, along with my alignment with Divinity. No Alignment, no Inspiration. No Inspiration, no Purpose.

In working with people, I'm always petitioning Divinity to transmute memories within my subconscious that replay as my perceptions, my thoughts, my reactions of them. From zero state, Divinity then suffuses my subconscious and conscious minds with Inspirations, allowing my Soul to experience people as Divinity experiences them.

In working with Divinity, the memories that get transmuted in my subconscious are transmuted in the subconscious of all minds, not just of people but of the mineral, animal, and vegetable kingdoms and all forms of existence seen and unseen. How wonderful to realize that Peace and Freedom begin with me.

Peace of I,

Ihaleakala

Well, I still didn't get it. I decided to ask if I could work with him, to write a book on what he does. It seemed like a logical way to get him to spill the beans about his method and to learn about his years working in the mental hospital. I said it would help others. I said I would do most of the work. I sent my e-mail to him and waited. He replied, saying:

Joe:

"Peace begins with me."

Humanity has accumulated addictive memories of perceiving others as needing help, assistance. Self I-Dentity through Ho'oponopono

(SITH) is about releasing these memories within our subconscious that replay perceptions that say that problems are "out there," not within.

Each of us came in with our "fore-bemoanèd moans" already made. Problem memories have nothing to do with people, places, or situations. They are opportunities to be set free.

The whole purpose of SITH is to restore one's Self I-Dentity, one's natural rhythm with Divine Intelligence. In reestablishing this original rhythm, zero opens and the Soul is suffused with Inspirations.

Historically, people who take SITH want to share the information with others with the intent that it will help them. Getting out of the "I can help them" mode is a tough one. "Explaining" SITH to people, on the whole, does not free up problem memories. Doing SITH does.

If we are willing to clean up our "fore-bemoanèd moans," we will be fine and everyone and everything else will be too. Hence, we discourage people from sharing SITH with others; instead, we encourage them to give up their stuff of others, setting themselves free first and all others second.

"Peace begins with me."

POI,

Ihaleakala

Well, I *still* didn't understand.

I again wrote back, asking if I could talk to him by phone. I said I wanted to interview him. Again, he agreed. We set an appointment to talk on the following Friday, a few days away. I was so excited that I wrote my friend Mark Ryan and told him the news, that I was finally going to speak to the mysterious Hawaiian shaman he had told me about years earlier. He, too, was excited.

We were both curious about what we would learn.

Little did we know what we would experience.

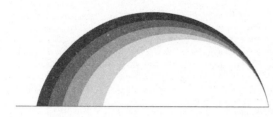

Our First Conversation

Every man takes the limits of his own field of vision for the limits of the world.

—Arthur Schopenhauer

finally spoke to Dr. Hew Len for the first time on October 21, 2005.

His full name is Dr. Ihaleakala Hew Len. But he told me to call him "E." Yes, like the letter in the alphabet. Okay. I can do that. "E" and I probably spent an hour talking on our first phone call. I asked him to tell me the complete story of his work as a therapist.

He explained that he worked at Hawaii State Hospital for three years. The ward where they kept the criminally insane was dangerous. Psychologists quit on a monthly basis. The staff called in sick a lot, or simply quit. People would walk through that ward with their backs against the wall, afraid of being attacked by patients. It was not a pleasant place to live, work, or visit.

Dr. Hew Len or "E" told me he never saw patients professionally. He never counseled with them. He agreed to review their files. While he looked at those files, he would work on himself. As he worked on himself, patients began to heal.

This became even more fascinating when I learned the following:

"After a few months, patients who had been shackled were being allowed to walk freely," he told me. "Others who had been heavily medicated were getting their medications reduced. And those who had been seen as having no chance of ever being released were being freed."

I was in awe.

"Not only that," he went on, "but the staff began to enjoy coming to work. Absenteeism and turnover disappeared. We ended up with more staff than we needed, because patients were being released and all the staff was showing up to work. Today that ward is closed."

This is where I had to ask the million-dollar question:

"What were you doing within yourself that caused those people to change?"

"I was simply cleaning the part of me that I shared with them," he said.

Huh?

I didn't understand.

Dr. Hew Len explained that total responsibility for your life means that *everything* in your life—simply because *it is in your life*—is your responsibility. In a literal sense, the entire world is your creation.

Whew. This is tough to swallow. Being responsible for what I say or do is one thing. Being responsible for what *everyone* in my life says or does is quite another.

Yet the truth is this: If you take complete responsibility for your life, then everything you see, hear, taste, touch, or in any way experience *is* your responsibility because *it is in your life.*

That means the terrorists, the president, the economy—anything you experience and don't like—is up for you to heal. They don't exist, in a manner of speaking, except as projections from inside you.

The problem isn't with them; it's with you.

And to change them, you have to change yourself.

I know this is tough to grasp, let alone accept or actually live. Blame is far easier than total responsibility. But as I spoke with Dr. Hew Len, I began to realize that healing for him and in ho'oponopono means loving yourself. If you want to improve your life, you have to heal your life. If you want to cure anyone—even a mentally ill criminal—you do it by healing yourself.

I asked Dr. Hew Len how he went about healing himself. What was he doing, exactly, when he looked at those patients' files?

"I just kept saying 'I'm sorry' and 'I love you' over and over again," he explained.

That's it?

That's it.

It turns out loving yourself is the greatest way to improve yourself. And as you improve yourself, you improve your world.

As Dr. Hew Len, or "E," worked at the hospital, whatever came up in him, he turned over to Divinity and asked that it be released. He always trusted. It always worked. Dr. Hew Len would ask himself, "What is going on in me that I have caused this problem, and how can I rectify this problem in me?"

Apparently this method of healing from the inside out is what is called Self I-Dentity Ho'oponopono. There appears to be an older version of ho'oponopono that was heavily influenced by missionaries in Hawaii. It involved a facilitator who helped people heal problems by talking them out. When they could cut the cord of a problem, the problem vanished. But Self I-Dentity Ho'oponopono didn't need a facilitator. It's all done inside yourself. I was curious and knew I would understand this better in time.

Dr. Hew Len has no materials on his process yet. I offered to help him write a book, but he didn't seem interested. There is an old video available, which I ordered. He also said to read *The User Illusion* by Tor Norretranders. Since I'm a bookaholic, I instantly jumped online and ordered it from Amazon. When it arrived, I devoured it.

The book argues that our conscious minds don't have a clue what is happening. Norretranders writes, "The fact is that every single second, millions of bits of information flood in through our senses. But our consciousness processes only perhaps forty bits a sec-

ond—at most. Millions and millions of bits are condensed to a conscious experience that contains practically no information at all."

As I understood Dr. Hew Len to say, since we don't have any
true awareness of what is happening in any given moment, all we can
do is to turn it all over and trust. It's all about 100 percent responsibility for everything in your life: everything. He says his work is
about cleaning himself. That's it. As he cleans himself, the world gets
clean, because he is the world. All outside of him is projection and
illusion.

While some of this sounded Jungian, in the sense that the outer
that you see is the shadow side of your own life, what Dr. Hew Len
seemed to be describing was beyond all of that. He seemed to be acknowledging that everything is a mirror of yourself, but he also was
saying that it is your responsibility to fix everything you experience,
and from the inside of yourself by connecting to the Divine. For
him, the only way to fix the outer anything is by saying "I love you"
to the Divine, which could be described as God, Life, the Universe,
or any number of terms for that collective higher power.

Whew. This was quite a conversation. Dr. Hew Len didn't know
me from Adam but he was giving me plenty of his time. And confusing me along the way. He's almost 70 years old and probably a walking guru to some and a nut case to others.

I was thrilled to have spoken with Dr. Hew Len for the first
time, but I wanted more. I clearly didn't understand what he was
telling me. And it would be really easy to resist him or dismiss him.
But what haunted me was the story of his using this new method to
heal so-called throwaway cases, such as mentally ill criminals.

I knew Dr. Hew Len had an upcoming seminar and I asked him
about it.

"What will I get out of it?"

"You will get whatever you get," he said.

Well, that sounded like the old *est* training of the 1970s: Whatever you get is what you were supposed to get.

"How many people will be at your seminar?" I asked.

"I keep cleaning so only the people ready to be there will be there," he said. "Maybe 30, or 50. I never know."

Before we ended our call, I asked "E" what the signature on his e-mails meant.

"POI means peace of I," he explained. "It is the peace that surpasses all understanding."

I didn't understand what he meant at the time, which, today, makes perfect sense.

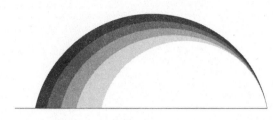

The Shocking Truth about Intentions

Our subjective inner life is what really matters to us as human beings. Yet we know and understand relatively little of how it arises and how it functions in our conscious will to act.

—Benjamin Libet, *Mind Time*

After that first call with Dr. Hew Len, I eagerly wanted to know more. I asked him about the seminar he was doing a few weeks later. He didn't try to sell me on it. He said he was constantly clearing so only the right people went to it. He didn't want a crowd. He wanted open hearts. He trusted that Divinity—his favorite term for the power bigger than all of us, yet all of us—would bring the right arrangement.

I asked my friend Mark Ryan, the man who first told me about Dr. Hew Len, if he wanted to attend. I offered to pay his way, as a gift for telling me about this miracle and miracle worker. Mark agreed, of course.

I did a little more research before the trip. I wondered if this therapist's method had anything to do with *huna*, a popular healing method from Hawaii. As I read, I learned it had nothing at all to do with it. *Huna* is the name that entrepreneur-turned-author Max Freedom Long gave his version of Hawaiian spiritualism. He claimed to have learned a secret tradition from Hawaiian friends while working as a schoolteacher in Hawaii. He founded the Huna Fellowship in 1945 and later published a series of books, one of the most popular being *The Secret Science Behind Miracles*. While fascinating, Long's work had nothing to do with the therapist I was investigating. As I was beginning to learn, the therapist was practicing something Long had never heard of, at least not in the way Dr. Hew Len practiced it.

As I kept reading and learning, my curiosity deepened. I could hardly wait for the day I would fly out and meet the healer himself.

I flew out to Los Angeles, met with Mark, and went to Calabasa, California. Mark showed me Los Angeles before doing so, and we had a great time. But we both wanted to meet the man we had heard so much about. While Mark and I had stimulating and deep conversations over breakfast, what we both wanted was the seminar.

When we went to the event room, we found a line of about 30 people. I kept trying to stand on my toes so I could see over everyone's head. I wanted to see the healer. I wanted to see the mystery man. I wanted to see Dr. Hew Len. When I finally made it to the door, Dr. Hew Len greeted me.

"Aloha, Joseph," he said, extending his hand. He was soft-spoken yet with charisma and authority. He wore Dockers, sneakers, an open shirt, and a business jacket. He also wore a baseball cap, which I later learned is his trademark.

"Aloha, Mark," he said to my friend.

There was small talk as he asked about our flight, how long it took to get from Texas to Los Angeles, and so on. I loved this man instantly. Something about his quiet confidence and grandfatherly style of being made me resonate with him.

Dr. Hew Len likes to start on time. As soon as the event began, he called on me.

"Joseph, when you delete something from your computer, where does it go?"

"I have no idea," I replied. Everyone laughed. I'm sure they had no idea, either.

"When you erase something from your computer, where does it go?" he asked the room.

"To the recycle bin," someone shouted out.

"Exactly," Dr. Hew Len said. "It's still on your computer, but it's out of sight. Your memories are like that. They are still in you, just out of sight. What you want to do is erase them completely and permanently."

I found this fascinating, but I had no idea what it meant or where it was going. Why would I want memories permanently deleted?

"You have two ways to live your life," Dr. Hew Len explained. "From memory or from inspiration. Memories are old programs replaying. Inspiration is the Divine giving you a message. You want to come from inspiration. The only way to hear the Divine and receive inspiration is to clean all memories. The only thing you have to do is clean."

Dr. Hew Len spent a lot of time explaining how the Divine is our zero state—it's where we have zero limits. No memories. No identity. Nothing but the Divine. In our lives we have moments of visiting the zero limits state, but most of the time we have garbage—what he calls memories—playing out.

"When I worked at the mental hospital and would look at patients' charts," he told us, "I would feel pain inside me. This was a shared memory. It was a program that caused the patients to act the way they did. They had no control. They were caught up in a program. As I felt the program, I cleaned."

Cleaning became the recurring theme. He told us a variety of ways to clean, most of which I can't explain here because they are confidential. You have to attend a ho'oponopono workshop to learn them all (see www.hooponopono.org). But here is the method of cleaning Dr. Hew Len used the most, and still uses, and the one I use today:

There are simply four statements that you say over and over, nonstop, addressing them to the Divine.

"I love you."

"I'm sorry."

"Please forgive me."

"Thank you."

As we went through this first weekend event, the phrase "I love you" became part of my mental chatter. Just as sometimes you wake up with a song playing in your head, I'd wake up hearing "I love you" in my head. Whether I consciously said it or not, it was there. It was a beautiful feeling. I didn't know how it was clearing anything, but I did it anyway. How could "I love you" be bad in any way, shape, or form?

At one point in the event, Dr. Hew Len again singled me out. He asked, "Joseph, how do you know whether something is a memory or an inspiration?"

I didn't understand the question and said so.

"How do you know if someone who gets cancer gave it to themselves or it was given to them by the Divine as a challenge to help them?"

I was silent for a moment. I tried to process the question. How *do* you know when an event is from your own mind or from the mind of the Divine?

"I have no idea," I replied.

"And neither do I," Dr. Hew Len said. "And that's why you have to constantly clean, clean, clean. You have to clean on anything and everything, as you have no idea what is a memory and what is inspiration. You clean to get to a place of zero limits, which is the zero state."

Dr. Hew Len states that our minds have a tiny view of the world, and that view is not only incomplete but also inaccurate. I didn't buy this concept until I picked up the book, *The Wayward Mind* by Guy Claxton.

In it Claxton writes of experiments that prove our brains tell us what to do *before* we consciously decide to do it. In one famous experiment a neuroscientist named Benjamin Libet hooked people up to an electroencephalogram (EEG) machine, which showed what was happening in their brains. It revealed that a surge of brain activity took place *before* the person had the conscious intention to do something, suggesting that the intention came from the unconscious, and *then* entered conscious awareness.

Claxton writes that Libet "discovered that the intention to move appeared about a fifth of a second before the movement began—but that a surge of activity in the brain reliably appeared about a third of a second before the intention!"

According to William Irvine, in his book, *On Desire: Why We Want What We Want*, "Experiments such as these suggest that our choices are not formed in a conscious, rational manner. Instead, they bubble up from our unconscious mind, and when they finally reach the surface of consciousness we take ownership of them."

And Benjamin Libet himself, the man who ran the controversial and revealing experiments, wrote in his book, *Mind Time*: "The unconscious appearance of an intention to act could not be controlled consciously. Only its final consummation in a motor act could be consciously controlled."

In other words, the urge to pick up this book may seem like it came from your conscious choice, but in reality your brain first sent a signal to pick it up and *then* your conscious mind followed with a stated intention, something like, "This book looks interesting. I think I'll pick it up." You could have chosen to not pick up this book, which you would have rationalized in some other way, but you could not control the origin of signal itself that was nudging you to take action.

I know this is hard to believe. According to Claxton, "No intention is ever hatched in consciousness; no plan ever laid there. Intentions are premonitions; icons that flash in the corners of consciousness to indicate what may be about to occur."

Apparently a clear intention is nothing more than a clear premonition.

The thing that troubles me is this: Where did the thought come from?

This is mind-blowing. Since I wrote about the power of intention in my book *The Attractor Factor*, and since I spoke about it in the movie *The Secret*, coming to realize intentions aren't my choice at all was a shock. It appears that what I thought I was doing when I set an intention was simply verbalizing an impulse already in motion from my brain.

The question then becomes, what or who made my brain send the intention? In fact, I later asked Dr. Hew Len, "Who's in charge?" He laughed and said he loved the question.

Well, what's the answer?

I confess I was still confused about intentions. I lost 80 pounds by being mentally tough and asserting my intention to lose weight. So was I declaring an intention or just responding to my brain's signal to lose weight? Was it an inspiration or a memory? I wrote and asked Dr. Hew Len. He replied, saying:

> Nothing exists at Zero, Ao Akua, no problems, including the need for intention.
>
> Weight concerns are simply memories replaying, and these memories displace Zero, you. To return to Zero, you, requires Divinity erasing memories behind weight concerns.
>
> Only two laws dictate experiences: Inspiration from Divinity and Memory stored in the Subconscious Mind, the former Brand-New and the latter Old.
>
> Jesus is purported to have said: "Seek ye first the Kingdom (Zero) and all else will be added (Inspiration)."

Zero is the residence of you and Divinity . . . "from where and from whom all blessings—Wealth, Health, and Peace—flow."

POI,

Dr. Hew Len

From what I could see, Dr. Hew Len was looking past intentions and going to the source—the zero state, where there are zero limits. From there you experience memory or inspiration. Concern about weight is a memory. The only thing to do is love it and forgive it and even give thanks for it. By cleaning it, you ensure that the Divine has a chance to come through with an inspiration.

What appears to be the truth is that my desire to overeat, which made me obese most of my life, was a program. It bubbles up from my unconscious. Unless I clean it, it will stay there and keep bubbling. As it keeps surfacing, I have to keep being aware of my choice: to overeat or not. This ends up being a lifelong battle. It's no fun. Yes, you can override the tendency to indulge by saying no to it. But obviously, that takes enormous energy and diligence. In time, saying no to indulging may become a new habit. But what a hell to go through to get there!

Instead, by cleaning on the memory, it will one day disappear. Then the desire to overeat will no longer surface. Only peace will remain.

In short, intention was a limp rag compared to inspiration. As long as I kept intending to do something, I kept fighting with what is. As soon as I gave in to inspiration, life was transformed.

I still wasn't sure if this was how the world actually worked, and I was still confused about the power of intention. So I decided to keep exploring.

I had dinner with Rhonda Byrne, the creator and producer of the hit movie *The Secret*. I asked her something I longed to know. I asked, "Did you create the idea for the movie, or did you receive the idea?"

I knew she had received the inspiration to create the now-famous movie trailer that caused a viral marketing epidemic. (See it at www.thesecret.tv.) She once told me that the idea for the movie teaser came to her suddenly and within a few seconds. She made the actual preview within 10 minutes. Clearly she received some sort of inspiration that led to the making of the strongest movie teaser in history.

But I wanted to know if the idea for the final feature movie itself came from inspiration or if she felt she did it for some other reasons. This was the crux of my concern about intentions. Were we stating intentions that made a difference or receiving ideas that we later called intentions? That's what I asked her as we sat together at dinner.

Rhonda was quiet a long time. She looked off, contemplating my question, searching within herself for the answer. Finally, she spoke.

"I'm not sure," she said. "The idea came to me, for sure. But I did the work. I created it. So I'd say I made it happen."

Her answer was revealing. The idea came to her, which means it came to her as an inspiration. Since the movie is so powerful, so well done, and so brilliantly marketed, I can only believe it's all the Divine unfolding. Yes, there was work to do, and Rhonda did it. But the idea itself came as an inspiration.

It's interesting that after the movie had been out for several months and the buzz for it was reaching historic proportions, Rhonda sent out an e-mail to all the stars in it, saying the movie now had a life of its own. Rather than stating intentions, she was answering calls and seizing opportunities. A book was coming out. Larry King was doing a two-part special based on the ideas in the movie. An audio version was coming out. Sequels were in the works.

When you come from the zero state where there are zero limits, you don't need intentions. You simply receive and act.

And miracles happen.

You can *stop* the inspiration, however.

Rhonda could have said no to the nudge urging her to make the movie. That seems to be where free will comes into play. When the idea to do something appears in your mind—coming from either inspiration or memory—you can choose to act on it or not, if you are aware of the impulse.

According to Jeffrey Schwartz, in his powerful book, *The Mind and the Brain*, your conscious will—your power to choose—can veto the impulse that started in your unconscious. In other words, you may get the impulse to pick up this book, but you can override that impulse if you want to do so. That's free will, or, as Schwartz describes it, "free *won't*."

He writes that "in later years he [Libet] embraced the notion that free will serves as a gatekeeper for thoughts bubbling up from the brain and did not duck the moral implications of that."

William James, the legendary psychologist, felt that free will took place *after* the impulse to do something and *before* you actually did it. Again, you can say yes, or no, to it. It takes mindfulness to see the choice. What Dr. Hew Len was teaching me was by constantly cleaning all thoughts, whether inspiration or memory, I would be better able to choose what was right in that moment.

I began to see that my weight loss came about because I chose not to obey the memory or habit that was nudging me to eat more and exercise less. By choosing not to follow those additive impulses, I was kicking in my free will or free won't ability. In other words, the urge to overeat was a memory, not an inspiration. It came from a program, not from the Divine. I was ignoring the program or overriding it. What I gathered Dr. Hew Len would suggest as a better approach is to love the program until it dissolved and all that remained was Divinity.

I still didn't quite understand all of this, but I was listening and choosing to not cancel anything out because it was new. Little did I know what was in store for me next.

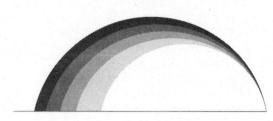

What Exceptions?

I am the story of what you think you see.

—Byron Katie, *All War Belongs on Paper*

The weekend event was deeper than I ever expected. Dr. Hew Len explained that everything you seek and everything you experience—*everything*—is inside you. If you want to change anything, you do it inside, not outside. The whole idea is total responsibility. There's no one to blame. It's all you.

"But what about when somebody gets raped?" a person asked. "Or what if there's a car accident? We're not responsible for all that, are we?"

"Have you ever noticed that whenever you have a problem, you are there?" he asked. "It's all about 100 percent responsibility for everything. No exceptions. There's no loophole that lets you off the hook for something you don't like. You're responsible for all of it—all."

Even when he worked at the mental hospital and he saw murderers and rapists, he took responsibility. He understood that they were acting from a memory or a program. To help them, he had to remove the memory. The only way to do that is by cleaning. This is what he meant when he said he never saw clients professionally in a therapeutic setting. He looked at their charts. As he did, he silently said to the Divine, "I love you," "I'm sorry," "Please forgive me," and "Thank you." He was doing what he knew to do to help the patients return to a state of zero limits. As Dr. Hew Len did this *within himself*, the patients healed.

Dr. Hew Len explained, "Simply put, ho'oponopono means, 'to make right' or 'to rectify an error.' *Ho'o* means 'cause' in Hawaiian and *ponopono* means 'perfection.' According to the ancient Hawaiians, error arises from thoughts that are tainted by painful memories from the past. Ho'oponopono offers a way to release the energy of these painful thoughts, or errors, which cause imbalance and disease."

In short, ho'oponopono is simply a problem-solving process. But it's done entirely *within* yourself.

This new and improved process was created by Morrnah, the beloved kahuna who taught her method to Dr. Hew Len in November 1982. Dr. Hew Len had heard of a "miracle worker" lecturing at hospitals, colleges, and even the United Nations. He met her, saw her heal his daughter of shingles, and left everything to study with her and learn her simplified healing method. Since Dr. Hew Len was also experiencing difficulties in his marriage at the time, he left his family, as well. That's not too unusual. There's a long history of people leaving their families to study with a spiritual teacher. Dr. Hew Len wanted to learn Morrnah's method.

But he didn't instantly accept her odd ways. He signed up for a workshop led by her and walked out after three hours. "She was talking to spirits and sounded nuts," he said. "So I left."

He went back a week later, paid the tuition fee again, and tried to sit through another workshop with her. He still couldn't do it. Everything she taught seemed so crazy to his university-trained mind that he again walked out of her seminar.

"I went back a third time and this time I stayed for the entire weekend," he told me. "I still thought she was crazy, but something about her spoke to my heart. I stayed with her until her transition in 1992."

Morrnah's self-directed inner method worked miracles, according to Dr. Hew Len and others. Her prayer somehow erased memories and programs just by saying it. I knew I wanted to learn that liturgy and would not rest until I knew it.

Morrnah hinted at her method in an article she wrote for the book *I Am a Winner.* "I have used the old system since age two, I have revamped the process, yet it retains the 'essence' of the 'ancient wisdom.'"

Mabel Katz, in her little book, *The Easiest Way*, says: "Ho'oponopono is a process of forgiveness, repentance, and transformation. Every time we use any of its tools, we are taking 100 percent responsibility and asking for forgiveness (for ourselves). We learn that everything that appears in our lives is only a projection of our 'programs.'"

I wondered how Morrnah's updated Self I-Dentity Ho'oponopono process differed from traditional ho'oponopono. Dr. Hew Len explained it this way:

Self I-Dentity through Ho'oponopono	**Traditional Ho'oponopono**
1. Problem solving is *intra*personal.	1. Problem solving is *inter*personal.
2. Only you and the I are involved.	2. A senior member mediates the problem solving session with all participants.
3. Only you are physically present.	3. Everyone involved in the problem must be physically present.
4. Repentance to the I.	4. Each participant is required to repent to each other, with the senior member mediating so that participants don't get contentious.
5. Forgiveness from the I.	5. Each participant is required to ask forgiveness of each of the other participants.

In traditional ho'oponopono, the senior member, trained in the dynamics of problem solving, is responsible to see that everyone gets a chance to say what each sees as the problem. This is always an area of contention in the traditional ho'oponopono because each participant sees the problem differently. I have to admit I like the new and improved process, as it all happens within the person. You don't need anyone else at all. This makes more sense to me. Since I'm a student of Jungian-based teachers such as best-selling author Debbie Ford (*The Dark Side of the Light Chasers*), I already understood that the place for change is within you, not the environment or any other person.

"Along with the updated Ho'oponopono process," Dr. Hew Len continued, "Morrnah was guided to include the three parts of the self, which are the key to Self I-Dentity. These three parts—which exist in every molecule of reality—are called the *Unihipili* (child/subconscious), the *Uhane* (mother/conscious), and the *Aumakua* (father/superconscious). When this 'inner family' is in alignment, a person is in rhythm with the Divinity. With this balance, life begins to flow. Thus, Ho'oponopono helps restore balance in the individual first, and then in all of creation."

He went on to explain more about this amazing process:

"Ho'oponopono is really very simple. For the ancient Hawaiians, all problems begin as thought. But having a thought is not the problem. So what's the problem? The problem is that all our thoughts are imbued with painful memories—memories of persons, places, or things.

"The intellect working alone can't solve these problems, because the intellect only manages. Managing things is no way to solve problems. You want to let them go! When you do Ho'oponopono, what happens is that the Divinity takes the painful thought and neutralizes or purifies it. You don't purify the person, place, or thing. You neutralize the energy you associate with that person, place, or thing. So the first stage of Ho'oponopono is the purification of that energy.

"Now something wonderful happens. Not only does that energy get neutralized; it also gets *released*, so there's a brand-new slate. Buddhists call it the Void. The final step is that you allow the Divinity to come in and fill the void with light.

"To do ho'oponopono, you don't have to know what the problem or error is. All you have to do is notice any problem you are experiencing physically, mentally, emotionally, whatever. Once you notice, your responsibility is to immediately begin to *clean*, to say, 'I'm sorry. Please forgive me.'"

As I researched Morrnah, even finding DVDs of interviews with her, I finally found the prayer she would say to heal people, whether she saw them or not. The liturgy she said went like this:

> Divine creator, father, mother, son as one . . . If I, my family, relatives, and ancestors have offended you, your family, relatives, and ancestors in thoughts, words, deeds, and actions from the beginning of our creation to the present, we ask your forgiveness. . . . Let this cleanse, purify, release, cut all the negative memories, blocks, energies, and vibrations and transmute these unwanted energies to pure light. . . . And it is done.

I wasn't sure how this unlocked the healing within someone, but I could see that it was based on forgiveness. Apparently Morrnah, and now Dr. Hew Len, felt that by asking for forgiveness we cleared the path for healing to be manifest. What was blocking our well-being was nothing more than lack of love. Forgiveness opened the door to allow it back in.

I found all of this fascinating. I wasn't sure how doing ho'oponopono could help heal me, you, or the mentally ill, however. But I kept listening. Dr. Hew Len went on to explain that we have to take 100 percent responsibility for our lives—no exceptions, no excuses, no loopholes.

"Can you imagine if we all knew we are 100 percent responsible?" he asked. "I made a deal with myself 10 years ago that I would treat myself to a hot fudge sundae—so huge it would make me sick—if I could get through the day without having some judgment of someone. I've never been able to do it! I notice I catch myself more often, but I never get through a day."

Well, now I knew he was human. I could relate to his confession. As much work as I've done on myself, I still get rattled by people or situations that I wish would be different. I'm far more able to tolerate most things that come my way in life, but I'm also far from being totally loving in every situation.

"But how do I get that across to people—that we are each 100 percent responsible for problems?" he asked. "If you want to solve a problem, work on yourself. If the problem is with another person, for example, just ask yourself, 'What's going on *in me* that's causing this person to bug me?' People only show up in your life to bug you! If you know that, you can elevate any situation. How? It's simple: 'I'm sorry for whatever's going on. Please forgive me.'"

He went on to explain that if you are a massage therapist or chiropractor and someone comes to you with back pain, the question to ask is, "What's going on inside of *me* that shows up as this person's back pain?"

This is a head-spinning new way of looking at life itself. It probably explains, in part, how Dr. Hew Len was able to heal all those mentally ill criminals. He didn't work on them; he worked on *himself.*

He went on to explain that at heart we are all pure, with no programs or memories or even inspirations. That's the zero state. There are zero limits there. But as we live, we catch programs and memories, much like some people catch a cold. We aren't bad when we catch a cold, but we have to do whatever it takes to clean it. Programs are the same. We catch them. When we see a program in another, we have it, too. The way out is to clean.

Dr. Hew Len said, "There is a way out of problems and disease for any individual willing to be 100 percent responsible for creating his or her life the way it is moment to moment. In the ancient Hawaiian healing process of ho'oponopono, the individual petitions Love to rectify errors within him. You say, 'I am sorry. Please forgive me for whatever is going on inside of me that manifests as the problem.' Love's responsibility then is to transmute the errors within him that manifest as the problem."

He added, "Ho'oponopono sees each problem not as an ordeal, but as an opportunity. Problems are just replayed memories of the past showing up to give us one more chance to see with the eyes of love and to act from inspiration."

Again, I'm forbidden to share the intimate details of the workshop. I'm serious. I had to sign a nondisclosure agreement. Mostly it was to protect the privacy of the attendees. But I can tell you this: It is about taking full responsibility for your life.

I know you've heard that before. So have I. But you've never taken it to the all-encompassing extent taught in the workshop. Complete responsibility means accepting it all—even the people who enter your life and *their* problems, because their problems are your problems. They are *in your life*, and if you take full responsibility for your life, then you have to take full responsibility for what *they* are experiencing, too. (Reread that. I dare you.)

This is a head-warping, mind-opening, brain-cramping concept. To live it is to transform your life as never before. But to even grasp the idea of 100 percent responsibility is beyond what most of us are ready to do, let alone accept.

But once you accept it, the next question is how to transform yourself so the rest of the world changes, too.

The only sure way is with "I love you." That's the code that unlocks the healing. But you use it on *you*, not on others. Their problem is *your* problem, remember, so working on *them* won't help *you*. They don't need healing; *you do*. You have to heal yourself. You are the source of *all* the experiences.

That's the *essence* of the modernized Ho'oponopono process.

Go ahead and chew on *that* for a while.

While you are doing so, I will just keep saying, "I love you."

One of the key points from this weekend workshop is that you are acting from either memory or inspiration. Memory is thinking; inspiration is allowing. Most of us by far are living out of memories. We're unconscious to them because we're basically unconscious, period.

In this way of viewing the world, the Divine sends a message down from above, into your mind. But if memories are playing—which they almost always are—you won't hear the inspiration, let alone act on it. As a result, Divinity doesn't get a word in. You're too busy with the noise going on in your head to hear it.

Dr. Hew Len drew a few illustrations to clarify his points. (See the State of Void diagram.) One was a triangle. He said that was you, the individual. At the core, there is nothing but Divinity. That's the zero state where there are zero limits.

From Divinity, you will receive inspiration. An inspiration is from the Divine, but a memory is a program in the collective unconscious of humankind. A program is like a belief, a programming that we share with others when we notice it in others. Our challenge is to clear all the programs so we are back at the zero state, where inspiration can come.

Dr. Hew Len spent a lot of time explaining that memories are shared. When you spot something in another that you don't like, you have it in you, as well. Your job is to clean it. As you do, it will leave the other person, as well. Actually, it will eventually leave the world.

"One of the most insistent programs in the world is women's hatred of men," Dr. Hew Len announced. "I keep cleaning and it is like pulling weeds in a giant field of weeds. Each weed is a leg of the program. There is a deep-seated hatred of men on the part of women. We must love it to let it go."

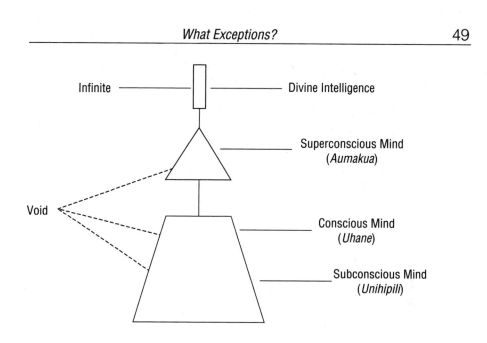

I didn't quite understand all of this. It seemed like yet another model or map of the world. Every psychologist, philosopher, and religion has one. I'm interested in this one because it appears it can help heal the entire planet. After all, if Dr. Hew Len can heal an entire ward of mentally ill criminals, what else is possible?

But Dr. Hew Len pointed out that ho'oponopono is not easy. It takes commitment. "This is not a McDonald's approach to life," he said. "This is not a fast-food drive-up window where you instantly get your order. God is not an order taker. It takes constant focus on cleaning, cleaning, cleaning."

He told stories of people who used the cleaning method to do what others might think impossible. One story was about a NASA engineer who came to him because of a problem with one of their rockets.

"Since she came to me, I assumed I was a part of the problem," Dr. Hew Len explained. "So I cleaned. I said 'I'm sorry' to the rocket. Later, when the engineer returned, she explained that the rocket somehow corrected itself in flight."

Did doing ho'oponopono influence the rocket? Dr. Hew Len and the engineer think so. I spoke to the engineer, and she said it was impossible for the rocket to correct itself. Something else had to happen that was in the nature of a miracle. For her, it was doing the cleaning with Dr. Hew Len's help.

I can't say I bought this story, but I also have to admit I don't have another explanation for it.

One man came up to me during a break at the event and said, "There's a famous Internet marketer who has the same name as you."

I didn't know whether he was kidding, so I asked, "Really?"

"Yes, he's written a lot of books and writes on spiritual marketing and hypnotic writing. He's a cool guy."

"That's *me*," I said.

The gentleman seemed very embarrassed. Mark Ryan had heard the entire conversation and thought it was humorous.

It didn't matter if people knew my celebrity status online or not, as I was getting known in the room itself. Dr. Hew Len called on me so many times during the event that people thought he was singling me out. One person asked, "Are you related to Dr. Hew Len?" I said no and asked why the person thought I might be. "I don't know; it just seems like he is focusing on you."

I never felt singled out in a negative way. I liked the attention and assumed it was to help me personally, since Dr. Hew Len knew I wrote books and had a following on the Internet. I'm sure a part of him knew that if I got this message of healing, I'd be able to help many people.

I didn't know at the time that he, being inspired by the Divine, was grooming me to become a guru. But not a guru to the world; a guru to myself.

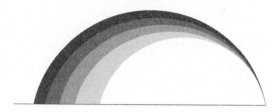

I Love You

You cannot be denied anything that is perfect, whole, complete, and right for you when you are your Self first. Being your Self first you automatically experience perfection in the way of Divine Thoughts, Words, Deeds, and Actions. Allowing your toxic thoughts to be first, you automatically experience imperfection in the way of disease, confusion, resentment, depression, judgment, and poverty.

—Dr. Ihaleakala Hew Len

absorbed Dr. Hew Len's message as best I could, but there was so much more I wanted and needed to learn. I've always been good at being a sponge and "getting" the ideas by just allowing myself to be open to them. As I sat in this first event, I began to feel that my sole job in life is to say "I love you" to anything that came my way, whether I saw it as good or bad. The more I could dissolve the limiting programs I saw or felt, the more I could achieve the state of zero limits and bring peace to the planet through me.

Mark had a little more trouble grasping the message of the seminar. He kept wanting to put it into a logical framework. It was becoming clear to me that the mind doesn't have any idea what is going on, so trying to find a logical explanation was in itself a recipe for failure.

Dr. Hew Len repeatedly stressed that there are 15 bits available to the conscious mind but 15 million bits happening in any one moment. We don't have a chance of understanding all the elements at play in our lives. We must let go. We must trust.

I admit that much of this was sounding insane. At one point in the event a gentleman said he saw a portal open in a wall and dead people float through it.

"Do you know why you are seeing that?" Dr. Hew Len asked.

"Because we had talked about spirits earlier," someone said.

"Exactly," Dr. Hew Len acknowledged. "You attracted them by talking about them. You don't want to look into other worlds. You have enough to do to stay in this moment in this world."

I didn't see any spooks. I didn't know what to make of those who did. I liked the movie *The Sixth Sense*, but as a movie. I didn't want spirits showing up and talking to me.

Apparently this is normal for Dr. Hew Len, however. He told the story of working at the mental hospital and hearing toilets flush at midnight—all by themselves.

"The place was filled with spirits," he said. "Many patients died in the ward in previous years but didn't know they were dead. They were still there."

Still there using the bathroom?

Apparently so.

But if that weren't odd enough, Dr. Hew Len went on to explain that if you ever talk to someone and notice their eyes are almost all white with a cloudy film around the edges, then they are possessed.

"Don't even try to talk to them," he advised. "Instead, just clean yourself and hope your clearing will remove the darkness taking them over."

I'm a pretty open-minded guy, but this talk of spirits and possessed souls and ghosts who use the toilet at night was a bit much for even me. Still, I hung in there. I wanted to know the ultimate secrets to healing so I could help myself and others to wealth, health, and happiness. I just never expected I'd have to walk through the invisible world and enter the twilight zone to get there.

At another point in the event we were lying on the floor doing exercises to open the energy in our bodies. Dr. Hew Len called me to him.

"When I look at this person, I see all the starvation in Sri Lanka," he told me.

I looked at her but only saw a woman stretching on a carpet.

"We have so much to clean," Dr. Hew Len said.

Despite my confusion, I did my best to practice what I understood. The easiest thing to do was simply say "I love you" all the time. So I did. When I went to the bathroom one evening, I felt the beginning of a urinary tract infection. I said "I love you" to the Divine while sensing the infection. I soon forgot about it and by morning it was gone.

I continued to say "I love you" mentally, repeatedly, no matter what was happening, good, bad, or different. I was trying to do my best to clean anything in the moment, whether I was aware of it or not. Let me give you a quick example of how this works:

One day someone sent me an e-mail that upset me. In the past I would handle it by working on my emotional hot buttons or by trying to reason with the person who sent the nasty message. This time I decided to try Dr. Hew Len's method.

I kept silently saying "I'm sorry" and "I love you." I didn't say it to anyone in particular. I was simply evoking the spirit of love to heal within me what was creating or attracting the outer circumstance.

Within an hour I got another e-mail from the same person. He apologized for his previous message.

Keep in mind I didn't take any outward action to get that apology. I didn't even write him back. Yet by saying "I love you," I somehow healed within me the limiting hidden program that we were both participating in.

Doing this process doesn't always mean instant results. The idea isn't to achieve results, but to achieve peace. When you do that, you often get the results you wanted in the first place.

For example, one day one of my employees disappeared on me. He was supposed to get some work done on an important project with an urgent deadline. Not only did he not finish, but he seemed to vanish from the planet.

I didn't take this very well. Though by then I knew about Dr. Hew Len's method, I found it hard to say "I love you" when all I wanted to say was "I want to kill you." Whenever I thought of my employee, I felt rage.

Still, I kept saying "I love you" and "Please forgive me" and "I'm sorry." I wasn't saying it to anyone. I was saying it to say it. I certainly didn't feel love. In truth, it took me three days of doing this process before I got anywhere near a point of peace within myself.

And that's when my employee surfaced.

He was in prison. He called to ask for help. I gave it, and I continued to practice "I love you" as I dealt with him. While I didn't see instant results, my finding inner peace was enough of a result to make me happy. And somehow, at that point, my employee felt it, too. That's when he asked a jailer to use the phone, and he called me. Once I had him on the phone, I was able to get the answers I needed to complete my urgent project.

When I attended that first ho'oponopono workshop run by Dr. Hew Len, he praised my book, *The Attractor Factor*. He told me that as I clean myself, my book's vibration will raise and everyone will feel it when they read it. In short, as I improved, my readers would improve.

"What about the books that are already sold and out there?" I asked. My book had been a best seller and gone through numerous editions, and was coming out in paperback. I worried about all the people who already had copies of my book.

"Those books aren't out there," he explained, once again blowing my mind with his mystic wisdom. "They are still in you."

In short, there is no "out there."

It would take a whole book to explain this advanced technique with the depth it deserves—which is why I am writing this one with Dr. Hew Len's consent. Suffice it to say that whenever you want to improve anything in your life, from finances to relationships, there's only one place to look: inside *yourself.*

Not everyone at the event grasped what Dr. Hew Len was talking about. Near the end of the final day, they started bombarding him with questions, all from the logical side of the mind, such as:

"How can my cleaning affect another person?"

"Where is free will in all of this?"

"Why are so many terrorists attacking us?"

Dr. Hew Len was quiet. He seemed to look right at me, and I sat in the back of the room. He looked frustrated. Considering that his entire message was about there being no "out there," that it's all inside you, he probably felt that everyone's lack of understanding reflected his own lack of understanding. He looked like he was going to sigh. I can only imagine that he was saying within himself, "I'm sorry. I love you."

I noticed that many people at the event had Hawaiian names, yet didn't look Hawaiian. Mark and I asked them about it. We were told that if you felt the urge, Dr. Hew Len could give you a new name. The idea was to identify with a new self on the way to having no self and merging with Divinity at zero.

I knew the power of a new name. Back in 1979 I became Swami Anand Manjushri. It was a name given to me by my teacher at the time, Bhagwan Shree Rajneesh. At that time in my life, when I was still struggling with my past, contending with poverty, and searching for meaning, the name helped me start fresh. I used the name for seven years. It was natural to wonder if Dr. Hew Len would or could give me a new name.

When I asked him about it, he said he checks in with Divinity. When he feels inspired, he says what he gets. A month or so after that first seminar, he wrote me:

Joe:

I saw a cloud come up in my mind the other day. It began a transformation of its self, churning slowly into soft, soft yellow. It then stretched its self out like a child upon waking into invisibility. From the invisibility the name **Ao akua, "Godly,"** surfaced.

I received this quotation as part of an e-mail message today:

"O Lord that lends me life, lend me a heart replete with thankfulness."

I wish you Peace beyond all understanding.

Peace of I,

Ihaleakala

I loved the name Ao Akua, but I had no idea how to pronounce it. So I wrote and asked for help. Here's what he wrote back:

Joe:

A is the sound for the letter a in father.

O is the sound for the letter in Oh.

K is the sound as in kitchen.

U is the sound as in blue.

Peace of I,

Ihaleakala

I was able to figure it out and enjoyed my new name. I never used it in public, but I did when writing to Dr. Hew Len. Later, when I began my blog online at www.JoeVitale.com, I would sign off using "Ao

Akua." Very few people questioned it. I loved it, though, because it felt like I was asking Divinity to clean my blog by using a phrase that meant, to me, the parting of the clouds to see God.

While the weekend training installed "I love you" in my head, at least temporarily, I wanted more. I wrote and asked Dr. Hew Len if he would come to Texas and talk about ho'oponopono to a small group of friends. This was my plan to have more of him to myself. He would fly to Texas for a small talk, and stay with me. While he was with me, I'd pick his brains about what he knows, including how he healed that entire ward of mentally ill criminals. Dr. Hew Len agreed and wrote the following to me:

> Joe:
>
> Thank you for taking the time to call me. You didn't have to and you did. I am grateful.
>
> I would like to propose to you an interview "format" for the informal visit in Austin in February. Perhaps the backdrop for the interview could be a kind of survey of problem solving approaches that you covered in your book, *Adventures Within: Confessions of an Inner World Journalist*. I see you being more than the interviewer and me more than the interviewee in this arrangement.
>
> Clarity is so important in conveying information, be it in whatever art form it takes. For example, there is much fuzziness as to what a problem is, much less its cause. How does one solve a problem when one might be unclear about it? Where is the problem to be found to be processed? In the Mind? What's that? Or in the Body (where most people put their bets)? Or both? Perhaps it's not in any of these venues.
>
> There's even the question of who or what does the problem solving.
>
> As you mentioned in your book, it is difficult to keep judgment at bay even as one attempts to problem solve using such methods as

the Option or Forum. Are judgments or beliefs the real problem? Let the real problem stand up for all to see.

The informal interview would not be about good or bad, right or wrong methods or concepts. It would be a way of teasing out recurrent unclarity. You and I would provide a tremendous service if we cleared the waters only one iota.

Of course, each moment carries its own peculiar rhythms and tides. In the end, as Brutus says (paraphrasing) in Shakespeare's play *Julius Caesar*, "We will have to wait till the end of the day to see how it all turns out." And so will we.

Tell me your thoughts about the proposed interview arrangement. I am not married to it as Brutus to the end.

Peace,

Ihaleakala

I quickly announced a private dinner with Dr. Hew Len and myself. I thought five or six people might show up. Instead, almost 100 people showed interest. And 75 people paid for a nice dinner to reserve their spot at the table.

Dr. Hew Len surprised me by asking for a list of everyone who would attend the event. He wanted to clean on them. I wasn't sure what that meant, but I sent him the list. He wrote back, saying:

Thank you for the list, Ao Akua.

It's only about cleansing, the chance to get clear of stuff and to be clear with God.

> Then, soul, live thou upon thy servant's loss
> And let that pine to aggravate thy store;
> Buy terms Divine in selling hours of dross;
> Within be fed, without be rich no more:

So shalt thou feed on Death, that feeds on men,
And Death once dead, there's no more dying then.

Peace be with you,

Ihaleakala

When Dr. Hew Len arrived in Austin and I picked him up, he immediately started asking me questions about my life.

"The book you wrote about your life (referring to *Adventures Within*) shows you did a wide variety of things to find peace," he began. "Which one really works?"

I thought about it and said they all had value but maybe the Option Process was the most useful and reliable. I explained it's a way to question beliefs to find out what is real.

"When you question beliefs, what are you left with?"

"What are you left with?" I repeated. "You're left with a clarity about choice."

"Where's that clarity coming from?" he asked.

I wasn't sure what he was getting at.

"Why can a person be wealthy and still be an ass?" he suddenly asked me.

I was taken by surprise with the question. I wanted to explain that wealth and "ass" aren't exclusive. There's nothing written that says only angels are wealthy. Maybe the obnoxious person is clear about money, so he can be wealthy and still be a cuss. But I couldn't find the words in the moment.

"I have no idea," I confessed. "I don't think you have to change your personality to be wealthy. You just have to have beliefs that accept wealth."

"Where do those beliefs come from?" he asked.

Having been in his training, I knew enough to answer, "They are programs people pick up from living."

He again changed the subject by saying I am truly a hypnotic writer. He was beginning to entertain the idea of a book by me about ho'oponopono.

"Are you ready for me to write the book now?" I asked.

"Let's see how the weekend goes," he said.

"Speaking of that, how are we doing this dinner?" I asked. I've always wanted to control the situation to be sure I do well and people get what they want.

"I never plan," he said. "I trust Divinity."

"But are you going to speak first, or me, or what? And do you have an introduction you want me to read for you?"

"We'll see," he said. "Don't plan."

This made me uncomfortable. I like to know what's expected of me. Dr. Hew Len was pushing me into the darkness. Or maybe to the light. I wasn't sure at that time. He went on to say something more wise than I knew at the time:

"What we humans are unaware of in our moment-to-moment existence is a constant, incessant resistance to life," he began. "This resistance keeps us in a constant, incessant state of displacement from our Self I-Dentity and from Freedom, Inspiration, and above all else the Divine Creator itself. Simply put, we are displaced people wandering aimlessly in the desert of our minds. We are unable to heed the precept of Jesus Christ, 'Resist not.' We are not aware of another precept, 'Peace begins with me.'

"Resistance keeps us in a constant state of anxiety and spiritual, mental, physical, financial, and material impoverishment," he added. "Unlike Shakespeare, we are unaware that we are in a constant state of resistance instead of flow. For each bit of consciousness we experience at least one million bits unconsciously. And the one bit is useless for our salvation."

This was going to be one fascinating evening.

He asked to see the room where we would be holding the dinner. It was a huge ballroom on the top floor of a downtown Austin, Texas, hotel. The manager was polite and let us into the room. Dr. Hew Len asked if we could be alone in it. She agreed and left.

"What do you notice?" he asked me.

I looked around and said, "The carpet needs to be cleaned."

"What impressions do you get?" he asked. "There's no right or wrong. What you get may not be what I get."

I allowed myself to relax and focus on the moment. Suddenly I sensed a lot of traffic, a weariness, a darkness. I wasn't sure what it was or what it meant, but I voiced it to Dr. Hew Len.

"The room is tired," he said. "People come in and out and never love it. It needs acknowledgment."

I thought that was a little strange. A room is like a person? It has feelings?

Well, whatever.

"This room says its name is Sheila."

"Sheila? That's the room's name?"

"Sheila wants to know we appreciate her."

I wasn't sure how to respond to that.

"We need to ask permission to have our event here," he said. "So I'm asking Sheila if it is okay with her."

"What is she saying?" I asked, feeling a little foolish asking the question.

"She says it is okay."

"Well, that's good," I replied, remembering that my deposit on the room was nonrefundable.

He went on to explain, "I was in an auditorium once getting ready to do a lecture, and I was talking to the chairs. I asked, 'Is there anybody I've missed? Does anyone have a problem that I need to take care of?' One of the chairs said, 'You know, there was a guy sitting on me today during a previous seminar who had financial problems, and now I just feel dead!' So I *cleaned* with that problem, and I could just see the chair straightening up. Then I heard, 'Okay! I'm ready to handle the next guy!'"

He's talking to chairs now?

Somehow I left my mind open to hear more about this unusual process of his. He went on to explain:

"What I actually try to do is teach the room. I say to the room and everything in it, 'Do you want to learn how to do Ho'oponopono? After all, I'm going to leave soon. Wouldn't it be nice if you could do this work for yourselves?' Some say yes, some say no, and some say, 'I'm too tired!' "

I remembered that many ancient cultures regarded everything as alive. In the book *Clearing*, Jim PathFinder Ewing explains that places often have stuck energies. It shouldn't be too crazy to imagine rooms and chairs having feelings. It was certainly a mind-expanding thought. If physics is right, that there is nothing but energy making up what we perceive to be solid, then talking to rooms and chairs just might be a way to rearrange that energy in some new, cleaner form.

But chairs and rooms talking back?

I wasn't quite ready for that at that time.

Dr. Hew Len looked out the window at the downtown skyline. The huge buildings, the state capitol, the horizon looked beautiful to me.

But not to Dr. Hew Len.

"I see headstones," he said. "The city is full of the dead."

I looked out the window. I didn't see graves. Or death. I saw a city. Again, I was learning that Dr. Hew Len used both sides of his brain in each moment, so he could see structures as metaphors and speak them as he saw them. Not me, though. I was just asleep in my shoes, with my eyes open.

We stayed in the hotel room for maybe 30 minutes. As far as I could tell, Dr. Hew Len walked around cleaning the room, asking for forgiveness, loving Sheila, and cleaning, cleaning, cleaning.

At one point he made a phone call. He told the person on the other end where he was, described it, and invited her impressions. He seemed to get confirmation about his own impressions. After he hung up, we sat at a table and talked.

"My friend says this room will let us do our dinner here as long as we love it," he told me.

"How do we love it?"

"Just say 'I love you' to it," he answered.

It seemed silly. Say "I love you" to a room? But I did my best. I had previously learned that you don't have to actually feel "I love you" for it to work; you just had to say it. So say it I did. After you say it a few times, you begin to actually feel it.

After a few minutes of silence, Dr. Hew Len spoke more words of wisdom:

"What we individually hold, memories or inspirations, have an immediate and absolute impact on everything from humanity to the mineral, vegetable, and animal kingdoms," he said. "When a memory is converted to zero by Divinity in one subconscious mind, it is converted to zero in all subconscious minds—in *all* of them!"

He paused before continuing:

"So, what happens in your soul moment to moment, Joseph, happens in all souls at the same moment. How wonderful to realize this. More wonderful, however, is appreciating that you can appeal to the Divine Creator to cancel these memories in your subconscious mind to zero and to replace them in your soul and the souls of all with Divinity's thoughts, words, deeds, and actions."

How do you reply to *that*?

All I could think was, "I love you."

Eating with the Divine

The Updated Ho'oponopono, a process of repentance, forgiveness, and transmutations, is a petition to Love to void and replace toxic energies with its self. Love accomplishes this by flowing through the mind, beginning with the spiritual mind, the superconscious. It then continues its flow through the intellectual mind, the conscious mind, freeing it of thinking energies. Finally, it moves into the emotional mind, the subconscious, voiding thoughts of toxic emotions and filling them with its self.

—Dr. Ihaleakala Hew Len

O ver 70 people came to the private dinner with Dr. Hew Len and me. I had no idea there would be so much interest in this unusual teacher. They flew to Austin from Alaska, New York, and other spots. Some drove from Oklahoma. I never could figure out why they all came. Some were curious. Some were fans of my books, such as *The Attractor Factor*, and wanted to take the next steps with me.

I still didn't know what to say. I still didn't know where to begin. Dr. Hew Len seemed comfortable going with the flow. He ate dinner at one table and everyone hung on his every word. The following experience is from my friend Cindy Cashman (who, by the way, plans to be the first person married in outer space; see www .firstspacewedding.com).

> *It was Saturday, February 25, 2006. I went to downtown Austin to listen to Dr. Hew Len speak. I sat next to him at dinner. His message is to be 100 percent responsible. I got to witness some powerful energy shifts. A lady at our table kept blaming a man for not calling the hospital when she had an asthma attack. Dr. Hew Len paused and said:*

"I am only interested in you and I heard that you need to drink more water and that will help your asthma."

Her energy shifted right away from that of blame to gratitude. I was so excited to witness this because I noticed how I was silently judging her by saying to myself, "She is into blame," and I find myself wanting to walk away from people who are into blame. What Dr. Hew Len did was take the negative energy and totally transform it into a loving, positive energy.

Next, I pulled out my bottled water. Pointing to the hotel water, I said to Dr. Hew Len,

"Their water is not very good!"

And Dr. Hew Len said to me, "Do you realize what you just did?"

When he said this, I realized right away that I had just sent negative vibes to the water. Wow! Again, I was thankful for becoming aware of what I was doing.

He was telling me how he clears himself all the time, meaning that when this lady was blaming the man, Dr. Hew Len asked himself,

"What's going on in me that this came up in her? How can I be 100 percent responsible?"

He sends his energy up to the Divine and says:

"Thank you—I love you—I'm sorry." He heard the Divine say, "Tell her to drink more water."

He also told me, "I know how to clear so she gets what she needs and I get what I need."

He talks to God and God talks to them. When I'm clear I will see everyone as God sees them.

I asked Dr. Hew Len if I could make an appointment to see him, and he said no because the Divine told him that I already had an inner knowing.

That was a beautiful confirmation for me to hear.

Overall, the message I learned tonight was:

1. *Witnessing how Dr. Hew Len transformed the lady's energy from complaining to that of gratitude.*

2. *Getting to see how I judged the lady and the water.*

3. *Understanding the system he uses to clear himself and how powerful that is for all of us to use.*

4. *To remember to say "Thank you" and "I love you" more often.*

I began the dinner by spontaneously explaining how I learned of the mystery therapist who healed an entire ward of mentally ill patients. I had everyone's attention. I invited people to ask questions as Dr. Hew Len and I held a public discourse, much like Socrates and Plato might have done, only I felt more like Play-Doh than Plato.

Dr. Hew Len began by saying, "People ask questions like, 'Well, what about beliefs? What about emotions? What about that sort of stuff?' I don't deal with those things. I don't deal with 'how come' kind of crap. But you are going to ask me that, so I have to deal with it! But it's like if I reach over and I touch something and it burns me quickly, immediately I lift my hand up. So, when something comes up, even before it comes up, I've already taken my hand off.

"It's like before I walked into this room—this room is sacred—before I walked in I made sure that I talked to the room. I asked the room its name, because it has a name. Then I said to the room, 'Is it okay for me to come into the room?' The room said, 'Okay, you can come in.' But let's say the room said, 'No. You're kind of—excuse the language—crappy.' So then I would get to look at myself and do what I need to do, so that when I come in, I come in as you hear that old phrase about physicians, 'Heal thyself!' So, I want to make sure that I want to come in healed, problem free, at least for a moment."

I interrupted him to set the stage for everyone. I wanted everyone to know who Dr. Hew Len was and why we were there. What we were doing was spontaneous and free-form. I advised everyone to relax and stay open. With Dr. Hew Len, you never know what will be said or done.

He asked everyone why someone would get breast cancer. No one could answer. Neither could he. He pointed out that there are millions of bits of information floating around at any moment but we aren't aware of more than maybe 20 bits at any one time. It was a recurring theme with him. But it was the essence of his message: We don't have a clue.

"Science has no certainty of what's going on in our life," he explained. "Even mathematics is unclear because of zero. In the end of Charles Seife's book, *Zero: The Biography of a Dangerous Idea*, the author concludes, 'All the scientists know is that cosmos was spawned from nothing and will return to nothing from whence it came. The Universe begins and ends with zero.' "

Dr. Hew Len went on to say, "So, I have taken the Universe of my mind back to zero. No data on it. You hear different kinds of ways of putting it: void, emptiness, purity. I don't care what you call it. My mind is back to zero now. No matter what is coming up, even when I am not even aware of it, the process I am going to talk about is *constant incessant zeroing*, so that I can be at zero."

I could see most people were riveted by Dr. Hew Len, but some were, like me, still in the dark. But Dr. Hew Len kept going, saying, "What happens is that only when your mind is at zero can creation take place, and it's called 'inspire.' In Hawaiian this 'inspire' is called *Ha*.

"So, if you've ever been to Hawaii, the word *Ha* means 'inspiration.' Wai is 'water,' and I is 'the Divine.' *Hawaii* is 'the breath and the water of the Divine.' This is what the word *Hawaii* is. The word *Hawaii* itself is a cleansing process, so when I am anywhere and I check—I say, for example, before I go into the room, 'What is it that I need to clear that I don't know? I have no idea what's going on, so what is it?' So, if I apply a cleaning process that is called 'Hawaii,' it will get data that I am not even aware of and take me back to zero.

"Only at zero . . . and something that you need to realize is the mind can only serve two masters one at a time. Either it will serve whatever is going in your mind *or* it will serve inspiration. This other stuff is called memory."

This was getting even more fascinating. From there, Dr. Hew Len went even deeper.

"Divine Intelligence is where all of this inspiration comes from, and it's in *you!!* It's not out there anywhere. You don't have to go over there. You don't have to go over there! You don't have to seek anybody out. It's already *in you!* The next level here is called the superconscious. That's simple enough. Hawaiians call this the *Aumakua. Au* means 'across all time and space,' and *makua* means 'holy spirit or a god,' which means that there is a part of you that is timeless and there's a part of you that has no bounds. That part of you knows exactly what is going on.

"Then you have the conscious mind; Hawaiians call it *Uhane.* Then, you have the subconscious; the Hawaiians call it *Unihipili.*

"So, one of the most important things to be aware is to question, 'Who *am* I?' So, what we are saying—what I am sharing with you— is that your identity consists of these elements of mind. Now, it is important for you to know that *this* mind is empty! So, this mind is *zero.* So, who are you? You are a Divine being—that's zero. So, why would you want to be zero?

"When you are zero, everything is available! *Everything!* So, now, that means that you are created in the image of the Divine. I'm going to be clear about this because I hear certain things, but I want *you* to be cleared by the Divine.

"So, you are created in the image of the Divine. That means you were created void on one side of the coin and infinite. As soon as you are willing to let go of trash and be empty, then immediately what happens is inspiration fills your being and now you are home free. You don't even have to know that you are home free, because most of the time you won't know. 'Where is it? Where is it? I've been clean! Come on, tell me where it is? I'll work more.' Most of the time you won't know!

"When the intellect gets hooked into being stuck, oh, it gets *more* stuck. It's what the Hawaiians call—excuse my language—*Kukai Pa'a*. Does anybody know what Kukai Pa'a means? It means intellectual constipation."

One person asked, "But if you have a challenge with another person, are you saying it's me, not the other person, who needs to be corrected?"

"If you have a challenge with somebody, then it's *not* with that person!" Dr. Hew Len declared. "It's that *memory* that's coming up that you are *reacting to*. That's what you have a challenge with. It is *not* with the other person.

"Now, I've worked with people who hated their husband or hated their wife. A woman one time said, 'I am thinking about going to New York. I'll have a better chance.' Then I heard the Divinity say, 'Well, wherever she goes, that's what goes with her!' "

Dr. Hew Len then explained that when someone contacts him for a therapy session, he looks at himself, not the person who called.

"For example, recently I got a call from the daughter of a woman who is 92. She said, 'My mother has had these severe hip pains for several weeks.' While she was talking to me, I was asking this question of the Divinity: 'What is going on in me that I have caused that woman's pain?' And then I asked, 'How can I rectify that problem within me?' The answers to these questions came, and I did whatever I was told.

"Maybe a week later the woman called me and said, 'My mother is feeling better now!' This doesn't mean the problem won't recur, because there are often multiple causes for what appears to be the same problem. But I keep working on me, not her."

Another person asked about the war overseas. He wanted to know if he was responsible for it. More exactly, he wanted to know what Dr. Hew Len was doing about it.

"Oh, I consider myself responsible!" Dr. Hew Len declared in no uncertain terms. "I do the cleaning every day, but I can't say I am going to do the cleaning and I want *that* taken care of. Only God knows what can happen. But, I'm doing my part, which is to do the cleaning, like clear out hospitals. We don't have a psychiatric hospital unit for people who kill people in Hawaii anymore. It's not there! I have done my part the best I could. Maybe if I had cleaned even more, there would be even better results. I am human and I do the best that I can."

I could see that Dr. Hew Len was getting tired and sensed he wanted to end the evening. It had been a remarkable time for all.

But it didn't stop that evening.

The next morning after our evening lecture and dinner, several people had breakfast together, including me, Dr. Hew Len, Elizabeth McCall (author of *The Tao of Horses*), and a few others. Whenever I'm around Dr. Hew Len, I begin to get quiet inside. I might be feeling the zero state. I might not. Who knows?

But at one point I had the sudden inspiration to hold a weekend event and call it something like "The Manifestation Weekend." I don't know where the idea came from. At least I didn't at the time. Now I know it was an inspiration from Divinity. But over breakfast, it felt like a good idea I didn't want.

I was busy with projects, travels, promotions, fitness contests, and more. I didn't need another to-do item on my plate. I tried to resist the idea. I decided to wait and see if it would just go away.

It didn't. It was still in my head three days later. Dr. Hew Len told me that if an idea is still there after several cleanings, act on it. So I wrote what became my most poorly written e-mail of my entire life and sent it to my database of contacts. To my amazement, one person called and registered for the event three minutes after I sent out the e-mail. She must have been sitting there in front of her computer, almost waiting to hear from me.

The rest of the sign-ups were just as easy. I wanted only 25 people for the event. It was my own self-imposed limitation, simply because I felt I could speak to 25 easier than I could to 2,500. Besides, I had never done this seminar before. In fact, I had no idea how to do it.

I told Dr. Hew Len about the inspiration and my concerns.

"My only advice is to not plan," he said.

"But I always plan," I explained. "I write out my talks, create power points, and have handouts. I feel better when I know where I'm going in my talks."

"You'll feel better once you trust the Divine to take care of you," he countered. "We'll clean on this."

By that I knew he meant that because the issue came into his experience, it meant it was something he needed to clear, too. Again, everything is shared. Your experience is my experience, and vice versa, once we are aware of it.

I did my best to not plan the event. I gave in to my fears at one point and created a manual to hand out to everyone. But I didn't use it and never looked at it. And no one cared about it.

I began the event by saying, "I have no idea what to do at this event."

Everyone laughed.

"No, really," I said. "I have no idea what to say."

They all laughed again.

I then proceeded to tell everyone about Dr. Hew Len, ho'oponopono, and how the statement "You create your own reality" means more than they might have thought.

"When someone is in your life that you don't like," I explained, "you created that. If you create your own reality, then you created them, too."

The weekend was wonderful. Even today, when I look at the group picture of everyone from that event, I feel the love we all shared. You can see this picture at www.BeyondManifestation.com.

But this was only the beginning for me.

I still had much to learn.

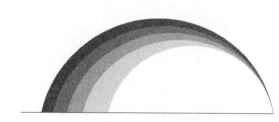

The Evidence

You must go into the dark in order to bring forth your light.

—Debbie Ford, *The Dark Side of the Light Chasers*

M any people had breakthroughs from the dinner and from the Manifestation Weekend retreat. In this chapter you can read their true stories, so you have a sense of the power of the ho'opono-pono process.

Here's one from Louis Green:

Dear Joe,

I want to thank you again for putting together the evening with Dr. Hew Len. Thanks are also in order to Suzanne for working on the details, including ordering me a vegan dinner from the Hyatt. I enjoyed sitting with you and Nerissa and getting to know both of you, as well as the other wonderful people at our table.

I felt privileged to have a front-row seat to hear Dr. Hew Len and for his grace and generosity in counseling me in response to my questions.

The two weeks following that night have brought me many amazing experiences, which I will gladly share with you. One thing that I had to remind myself of is that Dr. Hew Len sought clearance from the Divine to assist me, so that while I tried to apply ho'oponopono as often as I could remember, which turned out to be sporadically, I was still benefiting from his prayers.

I Received the Request for Dr. Hew Len Stories Right After Listening to the Recording

The first experience I will mention is the e-mail from Suzanne inviting stories and responses from the evening with Dr. Hew Len. Interestingly, I purchased Life's Missing Instruction Manual *and downloaded the MP3 recording of you and Dr. Hew Len. I had literally just finished another listening to the recording when I found Suzanne's e-mail in my in-box.*

My Lawsuit Went National with No Publicity

The second experience is pretty incredible. I had a new lawsuit to file before I left for Austin on February 23. I couldn't get everything together in time to make the post office before I left, so I mailed it the next morning from an Austin post office (February 24). Inexplicably, my materials got lost in the mail, and didn't arrive at their destination for filing until Monday, March 6.

I belong to a Listserv for consumer advocate attorneys from around the country. Last Friday afternoon, an attorney from Connecticut posted a capsule summary of a case that had been filed in Canadian County, Oklahoma, and asked if my colleagues in Tulsa had filed it. I almost fell over. It was my case. I e-mailed her back and called her office to find out how she found out about it. Then, I spent the next hour trying to find something on Google. No luck.

She e-mailed me back and said that she subscribes to an online service called Courthouse News Services (www.courthousenews.com), which has stringers (and probably moles) who monitor legal filings and opinions from around the country and report important, significant, or

simply intriguing developments. The one-paragraph synopsis★ appeared on
the front page, right column, of the web site, and I had sent out no
publicity on the case. Ironically, the client's father had visited my office
earlier in the day, and I had to reassure him that I believe in my heart
that we have a strong case to take to trial. It blows my mind to think that
out of thousands of cases that are filed every day, mine made the news.

A Dinner I Arranged at the Last Minute Attracted Record Attendance

I'm on the board of our local vegetarian group, and our monthly
meetings are usually on the second Saturday of the month. When I
checked with the president about a place for the March meeting, I found
out that no arrangements had been made. I volunteered to pick up the
ball. On Tuesday, February 28, I went to the top restaurant on my list,
only to find out that the owner was out of town until Friday, March 3,
but they'd leave a message for her to call me when she got back in town.
That wouldn't work.

    The next day, Wednesday, March 1, I went to a Thai restaurant
that had been open for only a few months. I spoke to the manager and
asked if they could do a vegetarian dinner buffet. I told him that based
on my experience, 20 people would be a lock, and a really good turnout
would be a little over 30. He said they could do it, but would want a
$100 deposit to make sure that they wouldn't take a hit if they bought
a lot of extra food and no one showed up. I picked the menu, and it was
an incredible deal: vegetarian sushi, soup, four entrées, dessert, and tea
for $8. He said he would check with the owner, and I'd have to arrange
for the deposit check. On March 2, we were able to confirm it. I wrote
a short announcement that the president could take and put into our

★Yukon Chevrolet and Fifth Third Bank have been sued for fraud in Canadian County
Court, Oklahoma, by a man of limited mental capacity who says he won a prize in
Yukon's "scratch and win" ad, and when he showed up to claim it, was detained for five
hours in a high-pressure sales ordeal and coerced into buying a new truck, which defen-
dants did not let him return the next day.

e-newsletter and e-mailed it to her. The dinner would be Saturday, March 11, and I requested RSVPs by Thursday, March 9 at 5:00 P.M.

Normally, our president gets the monthly newsletter out by a couple of days either before or after the first of the month. Most people get their newsletter by e-mail, and some get it by snail mail. We also post it at local health food stores and libraries. This time around, the president didn't have time to put out a newsletter, and basically sent out my e-mail to her as the announcement on Sunday night, March 5. The snail mail notices went out by postcard on Monday, and there were no public postings. I was beginning to think that we'd be lucky to get our 20 for the dinner.

On Monday, the RSVPs started to trickle in. I heard from a couple of people. A few more came in on Tuesday, so I thought we'd get the 13 minimum we guaranteed with the deposit. However, starting on Wednesday, the RSVPs came pouring in like never before. By the end of the day, we were up to 37. It occurred to me that we might experience a different kind of problem, so I called the manager and asked him what the capacity of the restaurant was; he said 65. The responses kept rolling in on Thursday, and by the time we hit our deadline, we were up to 55. I was not very productive at work that day because I was so excited and focused on checking my e-mail every few minutes (attractor factor?). I called the manager and asked if they could handle that many, and he said, "Sure."

I take a kabbalah class on Thursday evenings and didn't get home that night until after 9:00. I checked phone and e-mail, and received even more reservations. The count got up to 67. I began to seriously think about what to do with the overflow. My brilliant idea was to see if I could get the late responders who were begging to be able to attend to come a little later. More responses came in on Friday and Saturday. We got up to a stunning number of 75.

The event was a raging success! Not everyone who reserved attended, and a few showed up who didn't reserve at all (typical). The energy in the restaurant was awesome, as before long we had filled every seat in the place. This made a great impression on several people who had made the Thai buffet their first event. Some of the old-timers who were founding members over 10 years ago said that this was the record attendance for a Vegetarians of Oklahoma event. Staggering the seating worked perfectly. There were some who came for dinner and had to move on to other Saturday evening activities. There were always seats available for those who came later. The people at the restaurant were understandably pleased because they'd never had a group that large in before.

Rental Car Miracles

I rented a car to go to Austin because I didn't want to put the extra wear and tear on mine. I compared rates and figured out that I'd do just as well to rent a car for a week as just renting from Wednesday to Monday. I got a good price online to rent a midsize car, which I thought would be more comfortable than a compact. When I got to the rental agency, I found that there were very few vehicles on the lot. I did happen to notice that they had two orange Chevy HHRs, which have a cool "street rod" look. When I went to the counter, I was told that they didn't have any midsize cars to rent me. I asked if I could have an HHR, and they said that I could, even though they were classified as full size for some reason. I thought it would be cool to rent an orange hot rod to drive to Austin, since orange is one of the school colors for the University of Texas, my alma mater.

However, when I drove it off the lot and to my office, I realized that while the car was neat-looking on the outside, it was cramped inside with bad sight lines. I wanted to return it. However, I needed the car to get to my office and to run some errands. I couldn't get it returned during the day. I contacted the agency about swapping the car for a more conventional sedan, but they said that they still didn't have what I wanted on the lot, and that I'd have better luck in the morning.

I packed overnight and in the morning. When I went out to the HHR to throw in my suitcase, I discovered to my horror that the car had a noticeable door ding on the rear passenger's door. Of course, I always decline the extra insurance, and I didn't remember seeing the dent the day before, so I thought I was screwed. I thought that I'd go ahead and hang on to the car for a week and see if I could figure something out. I left much later than I wanted to, around 12:30 P.M. on a Thursday, and got into Austin around 6:30.

Fast-forward to Saturday evening at 5:00 P.M., an hour before I wanted to get to the Hyatt for the event with Joe and Dr. Hew Len. I had spent too much time worrying about the dent and what I was going to do. I was at a shopping center in North Austin trying to find a disposable digital camera, with no luck. When I got back into my car to drive back to my hotel, it was getting dark and there was a steady rain. I stopped at a place preparing to merge onto a busy street, when I felt a sudden smack. I had been rear-ended. Immediately, I was thinking, Oh shit, first the door ding, then this. I have a dinner in an hour that I've already paid for and I need time to shower and change. On top of everything, this was a high-traffic area, even on a Saturday evening. I got out of the HHR after first grabbing the rental registration information. A young black man met me in the street. "My tires," he said. "I've got to get new tires for my car. I couldn't get it stopped." Not a good thing to tell a lawyer, I thought. I said, "Crap, this is a rental car!" We walked to the back of the HHR to survey the damage. We both looked and were stunned. "There's no damage," the fellow said. "There's no damage. Praise Jesus!" Being Jewish, I thought that was amusing, but I looked myself and couldn't believe it. Incredibly, he was right—there was no damage. This car was apparently made with collapsible plastic. I knew that I was going to be sore, but I didn't want to stick around and make a big deal of this. I wanted to get back to my hotel. We shook hands and went our separate ways. I was able to make the dinner and sit at Joe and Nerissa's table.

I did some serious Ho'oponopono-ing about what to do about the door ding. I put off doing anything else about it until a couple of hours before I was supposed to return the car without penalty. I looked in the *phone book and found a place that did paintless dent repair. The guy at the shop gave me an estimate of $95, but it would take him a few hours to complete the repair. That would put me into a rental penalty, which I really didn't want to happen. I asked what to do, and the answer came clearly. Be honest. Call the local office of the rental agency and fess up. If they wanted to jam me on the repair, I at least had an estimate. I did call, and the guy on the phone told me not to have the car worked on, but to bring it by so they could check their records and survey the dent themselves. I said, "Fine." I took the car back and left it parked in the return lane. The customer service lady started scanning the bar code and taking readings on the HHR. I told her what was going on, and she sent me to the office/trailer. I found the guy whom I talked to on the phone, and he punched the car's identification number in on his computer. Miracle II: The damage was already noted on their records. I was not responsible. Hallelujah! I was home free!*

My Sister Was Offered Her Dream Job

My sister called one week after the evening with Joe and Dr. Hew Len. She's a vice president for a division of a very large, well-known company. She was contacted by a headhunter to find out if she would be interested in what she described as her dream job. She didn't want to tell me the details on the phone. Instead, she e-mailed me the job description she received from the recruiting agency. I was knocked over. Let's just say that the company is a luxury brand, and all I'd have to do is tell you one word, the company name, and that would say it all. A few months later, she was hired!

Here's another:

While I was attending a Landmark Forum three-day seminar in October 2006, Joe's shortcut to healing literally stopped the gushing waters. The nonstop gushing happened during the exercise called "being with people" or something like that. In order to "be with people" the seminar leader divided 74 people into four rows, and then we took turns, one row at a time, just being with people by looking them in the eyes without talking. I was in Row Three.

The seminar leader called Row One to step up onstage and face us, the audience. They looked at us sitting in our seats. We looked back. Then Row Two was ordered up to the stage and Row Two stood one foot away from (but facing) Row One. They were left looking into each other's eyes for three minutes. Then Row Two was asked to leave the stage and return to their seats. Again, Row One was left onstage to look at us in our seats and us to look at them onstage.

The closer it got to my time onstage, the more I realized I was stressing, but I had no idea why. My hands started to sweat and I noticed I also fidgeted in my seat. The task at hand seemed simple enough. I had always given great eye contact during conversations with strangers and friends my whole life. I would be just fine.

Then I remembered that at my first Landmark seminar the forum leader shared his story of when he first experienced this same exercise. He said that when he participated in this exercise as an attendee over 20 years before, his knees shook so hard that an assistant from the seminar placed his jacket between his knees to stop the noise.

Thinking back to what he said, I felt like leaving the room. I told myself that I didn't need to continue the exercise, that I was great looking people in the eye already! But I knew that leaving the room wouldn't be tolerated. So I stayed in my seat, sweating and fidgeting.

The first time my row was invited onstage was to stand one foot away from another row and look into their eyes. Whew! I don't have to look at 50 people. I just have to look at one! I thought. We got positioned and the seminar leader started guiding us through our three-minute process of self-discovery. Within the first 10 seconds I was crying uncontrollably, gushing water, and I had no idea why. I couldn't stop crying. Every time I looked at my partner across from me I just sobbed. "Row Three, please exit to your left," I heard. I said "Thank you" to my partner and left.

What the hell happened to me?! I was supposed to listen to what my inner voice told me, but I never heard a thing! I was just overwhelmed—no words. I didn't learn anything! What kind of exercise is this?! I was confused, embarrassed, and left to ponder my experience as the exercise continued on the stage in front of me. "Row Three, please stand, turn to your right, and go to the stage." *Aaaaaargh! Not again!* my mind screamed.

Now my row was facing the people seated offstage. I survived the three minutes this time because I just didn't look at people who were looking at me. Now Row Four was ordered onto the stage and a new partner was standing in front of me, one foot away from my face. This time I was face to face with a kinder older woman who smiled at me shyly. "Okay, I think I can handle it this time," *I told myself. But then the tears started gushing as soon as the exercise began. Each time I looked into my partner's eyes the tears just gushed and I turned away. She quietly tried to comfort me by telling me everything was going to be okay. I was embarrassed and confused by my unexplained tear gushes. The seminar leader was directing all of us to listen to what was inside our heads—what we said to ourselves. But my voice wasn't talking.*

Then I suddenly remembered that I could fill my head with thoughts instead of trying to listen to my thoughts. My inner voice wasn't talking to me, anyway. Once I put thoughts in my head that were better than what was there, I immediately looked again at my partner and thought, Thank you. I love you. Thank you. I'm sorry. I love you. Thank you. I immediately got comforted and was filled with appreciation and love for the woman across from me. I felt better and the gushing stopped. I was looking at her and I was not gushing tears.

To my surprise, my partner started crying. Tears started streaming down her face and her head started shaking slightly back and forth as she whispered, "Now you're making me cry." *I just kept sending her my private thoughts:* "Thank you. I love you. I'm sorry. Please forgive me. Thank you." *And so on. Then my partner was directed off the stage and I was left standing again in front of 50 people who were directed to look and evaluate me and my row. But now I was at total inner peace and I was able to look at people who were looking at me. In fact, I sought them out. I looked only at people who were looking at me. I felt so much better! I could be me with strangers! I loved everybody and really, really appreciated them.*

Soon the exercise was completed and the seminar continued; then we had a short break. The kind woman who had been my last partner sought me out and we talked about our experience. I told her I was obviously scared of people but I never knew it. She told me she felt like we really connected and went on to say that the seminar was helping her, too, because she realized she had a difficult time accepting love from others. Well, then it was obvious I had to share with her the healing technique I used to make me stop crying when we were onstage together. She started crying. We hugged and then parted to continue our short break.

Nerissa Oden
TheVideoQueen.com

Earlier this year, I discovered that an employee of mine had been taking larger sales commissions than she should have. This amounted to hundreds of dollars in loss to me and my small business. She refused to take responsibility for these actions. She is a hardworking employee who would not get another job in our small town making the kind of money she does with me. I had compassion for her, but I was also very angry and hurt. In the days that followed, I couldn't speak to her except about specific work-related subjects, and I could barely look at her. I didn't know what to do. I turned to Joe, and what happened next was truly amazing. He thanked me for contacting him. Then he gave me specific steps to take to clear the energy. First, I needed to understand that I attracted the situation—not easy to do, but essential to the process. Then I must forgive myself, the employee, and the energy surrounding the problem. Next I must set new intentions for how I want the situation to be and begin repeating Dr. Hew Len's healing words, "I'm sorry. Please forgive me. And I love you." The result was extraordinary. I wrote the following note to Joe after I completed the process:

Dear Joe,

Your suggestions were so right on. After I read them I had to drive from Wimberley to Austin, and I did each step that you laid out. It was simply amazing. I took plenty of time to understand that I truly attracted this and then forgave myself, my employee, and the energy surrounding it. I set new intentions and repeated that phenomenal Hawaiian healing method many times. By the time I reached Austin I felt like a ton of bricks had been lifted from my chest and stomach.

After I followed Joe's suggestions, the energy completely shifted inside of me. The anger and hurt were gone. It was truly amazing. The working environment with my employee is fine now. Suzanne, if anyone asks me if this system really works, I say it absolutely works!

Victoria Schaefer
Publisher, Pedal Ranch Publications
Wimberley, Texas

Here is a testimonial submitted by Denise Kilonsky, Shreveport, Louisiana.

This is a dream I was given in October 2006 that fits in perfectly with Ho'oponopono.

I saw a world without prisons because there was no need for them as a result of the philosophy of Ho'oponopono. The simplicity of the message of Ho'oponopono that was shared by Dr. Hew Len, Joe, myself, and others who practice it was being shared all over the world in programs and seminars. These programs taught people, especially young children, how to love themselves, and in so doing to love one another.

I saw myself in my dream teaching seminar after seminar attended by thousands and thousands of people. In these seminars I was inspiring people to remember who they truly are, their Divine nature, and what to do to be that person—to remember that their true nature is to love.

In this dream, I saw a teenage youth gang member pointing a gun at another gang member's head, threatening to shoot him. The youth under threat had just attended my seminar at his school. He kept talking about a miracle and wanted his tribe to experience the miracle, too. But they were sick and tired of hearing about it!

In this seminar, he remembered his true nature. *He was sharing his revelation with his fellow gang members and they felt threatened by his message because it was all too simple and it just seemed too easy and hoaxy.*

You see, in the seminar this young gang member had attended, he walked onto the stage and shot me in the gut. As I lay on the floor, my blood and life force flowing out of my body, I had the youth brought over to me and I embraced him and I whispered in his ear, "Please forgive me. I love you." And I died in his arms, embracing him with every ounce of love in my being. In that instant, the youth got the message. As he embraced my dead body, he whispered to me through his sobs and tears, "Please forgive me. I love you." In that instant, life force returned to my body and we were both filled with a beautiful golden light that was so powerful everyone in the audience and for miles around us could feel the love we two generated together.

As this love energy was noticed by those it touched, it grew larger and larger and spread out farther and farther. But not everyone was willing to notice yet. The young gang member this story is about, this young man who now held a gun to his own brother's head, was unwilling to notice and receive the love. The saved youth said to him, "Please forgive me, I love you," and embraced him and loved him as if he were loving and embracing all the darkest parts of himself.

And then it happened! The two were filled with the golden glow of love energy, and the other youth took the time to notice it and receive

this love he was being given. When he received it he said to the other,
"Please forgive me. I love you, brother. Please forgive me."

Guess what happened next?

The two were filled with a beautiful golden globe of love energy,
which grew larger and larger. As it filled the room and touched each
gang member—and they, too, noticed the love and received it—this
golden love energy poured out into the streets and for miles and miles
around. As others noticed, they passed it on and this golden love energy
grew and traveled farther and wider until the entire globe was filled
with love.

This is the Golden Age, the Age of Love. This is why we have been
given this gift of Ho'oponopono, to remember who we are and that our
true nature is to love. We all just want to be loved.

It's a beautiful dream, isn't it? The story of Ho'oponopono would
make a beautiful movie. I think of the movie Pay It Forward *and what*
an impact that is making in the world. The world is ready for
Ho'oponopono.

———————

Within the first seven days after I returned home from Joe Vitale's very
first Manifestation weekend, I could hardly count the number of miracles
that happened. Like a sponge, I soaked up all the energy, the lessons,
and the message, and my results continue to manifest at lightning speed.

To name a few of my tangible results: New clients flock to me.
New contracts seem to appear out of thin air. I've been approached for
countless joint ventures. My opt-in list has increased by more than
300 percent (at the time of this writing). I've been asked to make
a number of celebrity appearances, and I can hardly keep up with
all the amazingly inspired ideas that come to me out of the clear
blue sky.

To think, just three months earlier, I was an unknown in my industry.

All of this happened without force, without trying, and without any
real effort on my part. It has all quite literally flowed to me easily,

effortlessly, abundantly. When I get an inspired idea, I now take action immediately, and I am positively blown away by the results.

I have frequently used the ho'oponopono "eraser method" to grow my business exponentially, and I can't wait to see what I create next, as I continue to return to the whiteboard and clean, clean, clean.

Thank you, Joe and Dr. Hew Len!

Eternally grateful,
Amy Scott Grant
http://thesuccessmethod.com
http://newsuccess.org

Joyce McKee wrote:

During the past year, I took on a new role: I was a caretaker. My mother left her home of many years to relocate nearer her daughters, partly because of some challenges in our lives. Shortly thereafter, my sturdy, lifelong-rock matriarch was diagnosed with congestive heart failure and small-cell lung cancer. Wonderfully and gracefully, she chose to live out her remaining time with her daughters. She decided not to pursue cancer treatment at her age, 88 years old. So the medical professionals told us she would soon be out of time in this life.

The previous May, I attended Joe Vitale's Beyond Manifestation weekend and learned of Dr. Hew Len and his Ho'oponopono practice. I was intrigued. Hearing of the amazing results with the mentally ill criminals when he went inward to clean and clear himself impacted me greatly.

The universe is so gracious and provides the teacher when the student is ready. The timing was perfect. My main question that weekend was "How can I be used to help my mother in her dying process?"

I was willing to show up and acknowledge to the universe that I am 100 percent responsible for my life—all of my life, including

Mother. So I used what I had learned. I went inward and constantly cleaned and cleared.

The effects for my mother and me were simple yet exquisite. She remained clear of mind, pain-free, and able to take care of herself until the end. Yes, there were small crisis events when she needed the drugs supplied by Hospice; yet she was able to handle these situations in the comfort of home and was not rushed to the hospital. Those were transition-in-training moments, preparing us both for the final occasion when she would cross over to the other side.

The greatest gift was she lived on into "overtime." She lived well past the forecasts. Each morning she was surprised to wake and greeted me with a cheery "Guess what, I got another day!" We had time for all the words of love to be exchanged and for just casual time together. We had time to truly prepare for her transition. I came to experience fearlessness about the process of Mother leaving us. She knew where she was going and so did I. When we had those tense moments of labored breathing, we saw the grace of God and there was no fear. Wow, what a gift!

The Ho'oponopono practice, along with my prayers, changed the way I approach life. The feeling of empowerment I experienced and still experience is wondrous. To know that I can have an active role not only in my life, but also in the lives of others leads me to constantly, moment by moment, seek the Source of All.

Here's another:

When I attended the Manifestation weekend in May 2006 I was still feeling the emotional and financial pain of a $1.2 million contract that fell apart with a multibillion-dollar oil company midway into the contract. This was due to numerous internal issues in the oil company.

All the way home and for days afterward I said, "I love you. I'm sorry. Please forgive me. Thank you." A couple of days after arriving home I started feeling weak, sneezing, and coughing. I knew that it was my body releasing.

Shortly afterward, I had a discussion with a marketing expert, and during our conversation there was shift inside my body and in my perception of the entire situation with the oil company. He simply asked me what was the largest amount of money a client paid me in one year to help the client reduce pain in the workplace.

I told him $600,000, and then he said, "Wendy, you are there. You can use that to build an empire. How many people can make that claim?" In a flash I was able to see all the good instead of all the bad. Instead of only noticing the $200,000 they did not pay me, I was able to see the value in the $600,000 they did pay me.

I was able to see that focusing on the positive aspects turned on my passion, and this inspired me with ideas instantly. A light went on and I was in awe of something huge that had just happened inside of me. It was like there was light all around me that extended way out beyond my physical surroundings.

For two years I was the victim and angry with the people in the company who did what they did, and in an instant I was thanking them.

Shortly afterward, I developed pain in my left leg. I could not understand what had happened. I tried everything—massage, stretching, hot baths. Then I went to a Chinese medicine doctor who "read" my body and told me that I had been under a great deal of stress and that the pain was related to my gallbladder meridian—the anger meridian.

The energy was stuck and that was causing the pain. I was given four treatments of energy to release the stuck anger, and the pain left my body.

My body had been holding on to the anger I felt toward the big oil company, and when my perception changed it was ready to come out— only it got stuck!

Months after this experience, I discovered that my contact at the oil company who was instructed to break the contract with me refused to hurt another person and he quit his job. The department has been broken up and the services I provided are being handled in another department.

This energy clearing cleared the way for me to finish my e-book and launch my new web site at www.getinsideyourcomfortzone.com. The launch of the e book has created opportunities that I had not thought of.

It has been a dream of mine to teach the masses how to get out of pain from computer work. I am being given the opportunity to be the ergonomist for three popular web sites (so far), to answer questions about ergonomics, and to market my e-book, services, and other programs.

Perfect-size companies are calling me to consult with their employees to teach them how to get out of pain. The contracts are small and quick so that I have time to develop all the new inspirations that continue to come to me.

In addition, I am now teaching the Law of Attraction as a licensed and certified strategic attraction coach at www.theuniversallawof attraction.com.

The breakthrough I had shortly after the weekend was most definitely related to Ho'oponopono. It helped clear out the old to make room for the new. There is no other explanation.

Wendy Young

And here's another:

As an interventionist, one of the largest obstacles that I help clients eliminate or navigate through is drama. In The Celestine Prophecy *by James Redfield, the concept of a "control dramas" is defined: "We must face up to our particular way of controlling others. Remember, the Fourth Insight reveals that humans have always felt short of energy and have sought to control each other to acquire the energy that flows between people." Incorporating this concept into a more interventionistic model has allowed my own technique some intuition in cases where clients were distracted from their purpose or outcomes.*

Joe Vitale first introduced Ho'oponopono to me, though he may not actually know this. So on the one hand, I have the concept of drama or control dramas, and as an interventionist I require a balancing-out tool in order not just to understand a client but to assist the client back to full use of his or her resources.

"Getting back to zero" was the balancer I had not yet perfectly framed before Dr. Vitale led me into the world of Dr. Hew Len. In the Western world, especially the United States, our mainstream culture and its pervasive messages are all geared to get us to move from ourselves toward the flashy instant gratification of the consumer-crazy world we live in. "From zero to 60" couldn't be any more perfect as a catchphrase to define the emotional movement of a world addicted to consumption.

What Ho'oponopono has helped me understand is that healing and true fulfillment come from moving "from 60 to zero." So many metaphysical constructs include the idea of "detachment" but it never seemed like a complete or perfect concept to me. In some instances trying to achieve perfect detachment just seemed silly. Now, however, with getting back to zero I really grasp the dynamic of detachment and how to get there.

It's been 10 months since I had the good fortune to meet Dr. Hew Len at Joe's interview with him high atop the Hyatt overlooking the Colorado River. Much has been transformed in me and in my family's life. All my parents and in-laws are suddenly making huge shifts in their patterns and discovering they have manifested their dreams on a grand scale. My in-laws have purchased a half-million-dollar home to retire in that is one of the most peaceful places I've ever been (just down the road from Joe's house). My mother has worked through physical and emotional obstacles, only to find herself marrying again and being very excited about her senior romance. I've suddenly had a stream-of-income shift myself in a field that didn't allow me to cultivate and demonstrate my greatest strengths. My father (72 years young) has finally broken an income chain that had him commuting from Houston to Prudhoe Bay, Alaska (fifth most northern town in the world) every six weeks. One of my oldest friends has completely uprooted a very set-in-his-ways life and come to Austin where he is currently developing his own company and living a totally different paradigm. My brother-in-law is finally moving into his own home. My sister-in-law and her husband are moving from the suburbs onto a dream property themselves. My godniece, who just started high school this year, has already been in a prime-time TV series and was nominated as Homecoming Queen. And her mother has just been offered the most lucrative business opportunity of her life. All this has started and been brought to fruition since February 2006, when I first heard about Ho'ponopono. Suddenly my day-to-day living is filled with experiences that are colorful and fun again after having spent the past 17 years being serious and dreary.

Life is a habit, so I've been acquiring the habit of a good life.

I'm not in any way an expert on Ho'oponopono. It is still very new to me and I will not predict where it leads my life experience. I am grateful for Dr. Vitale revealing the world of Ho'oponopono through the presentation that Dr. Hew Len made those short months ago. Whether it be in my personal life with my beautiful wife or in my business life, reaching the zero state, 100 percent responsibility, apology, and forgiveness are powerful choices that have made a powerful impact in my life. Thank you, Joe, and thank you, Dr. Hew Len.

Bruce Burns
www.YourOwnBestGood.com

Dear Joe,
I wanted to give you a great big thank-you for bringing Dr. Hew Len to Austin. The program was wonderful, leaving me filled with new understanding about life and how universal laws govern our health and happiness. Please allow me to expand.

First off, I want to say that I am certainly not an expert on the practice of Ho'oponopono. So please forgive me if I'm reading too much into what was shared, but here's what I walked away with after just one evening's experience.

Dr. Hew Len talked a lot about something very dear to my heart—the art of going to zero. In fact, this seems to be a centerpiece of Ho'oponopono. Being a martial artist and qigong teacher for many years now, I have come to regard this ability of cleaning and emptying the mind (going to zero) as one of the greatest gifts known to mankind.

Dr. Hew Len reminded us of the importance of living in a state of openness, cleansing our internal reactions, and going to zero. I was in complete agreement with his outlook on life and thrilled to meet another human being on this planet who shares about truths I have come to love.

In the art and practice of qigong (internal martial art energy exercise), there is a very specific way to breathe and circulate our body's internal energy. The ancient martial arts masters have discovered that there are universal laws working within our bodies and when we learn how to move our internal energy in a circular fashion we can create high levels of vibrant health and profoundly raise our consciousness. This process is often referred to as the microcosmic orbit.

(Fundamentally put—we breathe in and direct the life-force energy inside the breath down the front of our body into the lower belly region (an area known as the Dan Tien). Next we direct the energy up our spine and finally back around to the front. This ongoing process creates a microcosmic orbit within our energy-body, uplifting our health and our consciousness.)

When Dr. Hew Len used a diagram to explain Ho'oponopono and show how communication and consciousness between people best flow in a circular direction, I was immediately struck by its similarity to the microcosmic orbit. In fact, it was off-the-charts exciting to see how the universe works with circles in a way I'd never realized before.

Through the diagram he drew I finally understood how most of the time we try to relate to people in a bidirectional, linear fashion. We talk at each other; we argue, negotiate, point the finger, and so on—and this all takes place in a horizontal direction.

However, I saw that by moving in an entirely different direction, we could effect the greatest change and the deepest connection with another human being—and that direction was a circle. For me, Dr. Hew Len's diagram showed that by first going to zero—down beneath the conscious layer of the mind—we can let go of our reactions and attachments to what we are perceiving. We can then begin to rise up toward the superconscious state and eventually tap into Divine awareness. The Divine can carry our clear and loving intention down toward the other person, basically sneaking in the backdoor of their conscious mind, allowing for a pure and unfiltered connection and relating.

All I can say is it works like nothing else ever has. For example, just last week I was in a business meeting and the person on the other side of the table was asking for things that I initially felt were unfair and selfish. I caught myself tightening up within, and I remembered the diagram and the benefit of the circular direction, so I decided to stop fighting and I just let go.

First I connected to my breath and went to zero. Internally, I felt my awareness lifting up (just like the qigong exercise that I described earlier) and my disposition changed immediately. If I had spoken what I was feeling inside it would have been, "I love and support you. Please forgive me for being hard with you. How can I help you to feel safe and help both of us get what we are wanting?"

Next something amazing happened: My friend (I was no longer seeing the person as an enemy or a threat) began to change, becoming much more open and receptive as if having stopped struggling with some internal conflict. Within 15 minutes we even came up with a solution to our previous dilemma, a solution that was perfect for us both—and one that I never could have conceived of in my previous state of mind.

As the mysteries of life unfold, you begin to see how everything is connected; everything comes from universal laws, and one of those laws is circles. In the movie The Secret, *I remember you said that "the universe likes speed." I would like to add that the universe likes circles, too, ☺ ☺ and life certainly flows all the more smoothly when you know in which direction the circle wants to go.*

So thank you again, Joe. The diagram Dr. Hew Len used to explain Ho'oponopono has been so helpful. Seeing this process in a diagram has given me a great insight and a wonderful tool to catch when I am forcing things versus letting go and responding to situations from a state of zero.

Warmly,
Nick "Tristan" Truscott, Sensei
www.SenseiTristan.com
www.AllWaysZen.com

———————

Every day since the May Manifestation weekend I say, "I love you, I'm sorry, forgive me, thank you."

Nothing much has changed that can be easily observed, cataloged, or cheered, as I have, currently, a marvelous life.

Of course, I would like a bundle of wealth so I could easily visit my daughters and family in Queensland and my brother in Paris, and take my husband on the train ride of his dreams. And I'd like my novels to entertain the world. But these would be minor gifts compared to what I have now.

The invisible change is incredible. When I say, "I'm sorry," I truly do feel responsible for whatever is in my consciousness at the moment. I can no longer separate myself from people who disagree with me.

I have never felt so connected.

I am sorry for what I am doing in Iraq, for one. I hate to make phone calls but I am making phone calls all over the country in case I can change what I am doing in Iraq. It helps me heal.

Because I feel forgiven, I am so very grateful.

BLACKOUT ON DEER CANYON ROAD

Late afternoon—sudden silence
The absence of electrical humming

can be humanizing
I felt electrically alive

No power in any room
in any house
up and down the street
No news of restoration

We bathed in the hot tub
dined outdoors on wine and cheese
conversed in hushed tones
and watched stars

A blackout on Deer Canyon Road
in Arroyo Grande, California—
unusual, luxurious—so not like
a blackout in Buffalo or Baghdad

Evelyn Cole
The Whole-Mind Writer
http://write-for-wealth.com

———

After I learned about Ho'oponopono from Dr. Hew Len and Dr. Vitale, I found out that my business is about constantly cleansing. When I cleanse and get back to zero, business runs smoothly. I'm constantly clearing and constantly getting back to zero, and Dr. Hew Len taught me how to do that.

I took a business colleague to meet Dr. Hew Len and Dr. Vitale and found we have so much in common that we went out on a date that same night. Eight months later we are more in love than ever. The key is to be with like-minded people and to forgive and transform. Thank you, Dr. Hew Len and Dr. Vitale, for bringing Ho'oponopono to a larger audience. Also thanks for being the perfect meeting place to meet my love of my life.

Chris "The Prosperity Guy" Stewart
www.TheProsperityGuy.com

———

The drive to Austin felt like a vacation after months on the road with the show. Leaving Houston behind was more than a 24-hour break from the all-encompassing universe of a production on tour. It was the juncture of a night of reckoning that would reorder my reality even before the dinner presentation that Dr. Joe Vitale was hosting began.

It had been months since I'd last listened to one of Dr. Ihaleakala Hew Len's Ho'oponopono presentations—a year and a half to be exact. Even though I'd never met Joe Vitale before, I felt grateful for the fact he had brought Ihaleakala to a location within driving distance and I could be part of the event in Austin.

As changing scenery and little Texas towns skimmed by the car window en route to Austin, thoughts of other Ho'oponopono presentations surfaced and things I'd forgotten came back to mind. I flashed back to the first of many times I'd heard Ihaleakala speak and had gotten chills down my spine when he read the Opening Prayer in Hawaiian. I remembered how I'd landed a book contract two weeks after taking my first Ho'oponopono training, virtually by just showing up at a publishers convention, talking and leaving my card. Two days later a publisher called and asked me to submit ideas for a book they were doing. I had the contract by the end of the month.

As the distance to Austin grew shorter, I also reflected on a time just six months earlier when a veterinarian in Montreal conveyed the sad news that my dear cat Maya had intestinal lymphoma. It was questionable whether she would live long enough for me to take her from the clinic. When Maya was released, the vet thought that with luck, I'd have a few weeks to "tell her good-bye." I contacted Ihaleakala for help with a special cleaning, something to clean whatever this precious little creature had taken on of mine. It is now a year and three months since Maya's diagnosis. Little could I have imagined at the moment I was prepared for her imminent departure that months and miles later she would still be with me on tour.

Seeing Ihaleakala again in Austin was like breaking through the surface after being underwater—one of those "back in the world" kind of experiences. Yet it was also immediate immersion into the most profound life-altering practice I have experienced in 25 years of delving into everything from Buddhism, Celtic spiritual traditions, traditional psychotherapy, dream analysis (and I was good at that), energy work, and even Wicca.

And there I was in Austin, face to face with Ho'oponopono again, a philosophy, a tradition, that virtually wipes the slate clean of the practices, procedures, and endless analytical activities I'd so diligently studied for so long before it—all in an effort to understand, fix myself, and live the life I came here to live. I have to admit, there was a part of me that was ready to jump right in among those who'd never encountered Ho'oponopono before and let them know "I already do that," but I started cleaning and the nonsense (memories) dispersed.

Before Dr. Vitale had even introduced Ihaleakala that evening, a revelation hit me like a bolt of lightning, causing me to jump up from the table where I was sitting and run to the ladies' room, choking back tears. In that moment in Austin, in a room that looked out on the downtown skyline, Ho'oponopono enveloped my being and I had a moment of clarity when I knew I no longer wanted to be on tour, no matter what. Six weeks later, Maya the cat and I were heading west en route to Los Angeles, bound for a new home in Topanga Canyon that surfaced just in time for our arrival when the person who was going to take it suddenly decided not to rent it.

Another seven months have passed and just last week as I wavered on the edge of yet another significant change, I read a phrase that Ihaleakala wrote: "Zero is home base." I cleaned and stepped off the edge of another existence as I'd known it and now can say that I didn't fall.

Thank you for this opportunity to share the changes, revelations, and reflections about Ho'oponopono that surfaced from my trip to Austin in February.

POI
Elizabeth Kaye McCall

Before learning about and applying the method, I was experiencing struggle in many areas of my life: a husband who didn't believe in me and my ability to build a thriving practice, a practice that was far from successful, and a feeling that I was all alone in pursuit of bigger dreams and goals.

During the weekend with Joe when I learned the method, I met a young woman who had similar interests and goals and we agreed to do a business venture together. That venture was extremely successful and took my practice from limping to thriving in just two months. We are working on our next project. I feel as if we've been close friends for years and not months. The best and most significant change is that even before my business took off, the relationship with my husband changed in just a few weeks. I had been using the method whenever I experienced discomfort with my relationship and suddenly my husband was rereading my e-books, asking me questions, and sharing his own experiences. He took on more responsibility at work and has a renewed sense of pride and love for himself, which has a sizzling impact on our relationship!

I have an unwavering trust and confidence in myself and what unfolds before me, all the while just doing a simple method in minutes a day.

Thank you!

Karrie King
Author of The Red Hot Bedroom *(www.redhotbedroom.com)*
Creator of Joyful Spaces *(www.joyfulspaces.com)*

———

Ho'oponopono Goes Back through Time

I'm an animal lover.

A huge one.

I don't care or worry only about my own—I love them all.

Years ago, a friend of mine turned me on to The Animal Rescue Site *at www.theanimalrescuesite.com.*

You can fund food for animals in sanctuaries by going to this site and clicking on the "Feed an Animal in Need" button. Every click provides .6 bowls of food to the hungry. A click per day is all it takes to make a difference. I've been visiting this site for the past five years, every day, without fail.

One Saturday morning, I was cleaning out my e-mails and feeling good about doing my part in the world—"feeding the animals in need." I happened to notice a picture listed by one of the site's sponsors.

What I saw was an animal in a cage trying to eat its way through the bars. It looked so sickly and gaunt that not even all that beautiful fluffy fur could mask its pain. In fact, it looked so terribly tortured that I couldn't even make out what kind of animal it was! Was it a bear? A raccoon? I honestly couldn't tell. Truthfully, I didn't want to look closer. My fear told me that I would only be reminding myself how much pain exists in the world and that there was very little I could do about it. Still, I know better than to look the other way just so that I can feel better.

I felt this overwhelming need to tune in. I could hear the animal calling to me, asking me to wake up and pay attention. As I looked closer, to my horror I discovered that what I was seeing were captured bears, held in their cages for tens of years on end.

> The bears live in cages little bigger than themselves for ease of "milking." Bile is extracted through a cut made in the bear's abdomen and into the gallbladder, where bile is stored after being secreted by the liver via the hepatic duct. A tube is inserted into this opening to tap the bile, or a steel stick is forced into the gallbladder with the bile then running down it into a basin. Between 10 and 20 ml of bile is tapped from each bear twice daily. The WSPA [World Society for the Protection of Animals] reports that, during milking, investigators saw bears moaning, banging their heads against their cages, and chewing their own paws. The mortality rate is between 50 and 60 percent. When the bears stop producing bile after a few years, they are moved to another cage, where they either are left to starve to death or are killed for their paws and gallbladders. Bear paws are considered a delicacy. (http://en.wikipedia.org/wiki/Bile_bear)

I felt completely sick to my stomach and had a knee-jerk reaction to unleash my anger toward these ignorant poachers. It took all the discipline I had to remind myself that shame and blame never change a person and that thankfully, thanks to Dr. Joe and Dr. Hew Len, I now had something much better in my bag of tricks that I could apply: Ho'oponopono.

I began to recite the phrases, "I'm sorry. Please forgive me. I love you. Thank you." As I repeated the mantra over and over and over again, I visualized the bear farmers' hearts being filled with love, understanding, and compassion. I saw them having their own "lightbulb moment" as my information passed through them and they got in touch with their own awareness. With their level of consciousness being raised and no one to blame for the blood on their hands but themselves, I imagined them falling to their knees in complete agony—begging and pleading with God and the bears to grant them mercy and forgiveness for the torture and suffering they've caused these beautiful creatures. Then, I saw them releasing all the bears and providing them with the medicine, care, and healing that they were in dire need of and finally setting them free again.

Many of you don't know (as I didn't know) that bear bile has been used for centuries. Today it is used in wine, shampoo, and medicine. The enormous weight behind this tragedy didn't solely involve healing the present moment—my clearing work occupied going back through time, through the ages. There was hundreds of years' worth of pain here to heal.

This experience consumed me. For hours that day, I couldn't focus on anything else and kept repeating: "I'm sorry. Please forgive me. Thank you. I love you."

The heaviness of this global pain was inescapable and undeniable. I was consumed with anguish. And I was grieving. It was as if I was the one who captured those bears and held the key to their prison myself.

Once a week, my husband and I make it a point to have a "date day." On this day he invited me to go see a movie with him. I was in

*agony and didn't feel much like going out. But I knew it wouldn't
make any sense to say, "No thanks. I'm really not up to it—I'm
worried about the bears."*

*Keeping my own clearing work to myself, I agreed to go out with
him. We went to see the movie 16 Blocks with Bruce Willis. Little did
I know then that the theme of this movie would be in complete
alignment with what I was already experiencing. The highlighted
message in the movie was "People can change."*

*All throughout the movie, I practiced Ho'oponopono. In one scene,
I noticed a bus in the background and the banner/ad on the side of the
bus showed a picture of a teddy bear and the words beneath the bear
read: "Send Love."*

*My previous training would reveal to me that this was a "waking
dream." My current teachings would say, "Keep doing what you're
doing. You're on the right track!" Is this how the universe speaks to us?
I'd like to think so.*

*It was yet another reminder to me that the bear farmers didn't need
my anger to change; they just needed my love. The bears needed my
love. The world needs our love. Love changes people and there are no
exceptions to this rule. Sending love to a dangerous, ugly, or abusive
situation is the only thing we can do if we're looking for drama-free
healing and everlasting change. It's not always an easy thing to do, but
herein forever lies the answer: love.*

*As my hypervigilance started to quiet down and the day faded into
evening, the nausea, anxiety, guilt, pain, and grief that I was feeling
earlier were finally starting to subside. Still, I continued to
Ho'oponopono my way throughout the remainder of the day until I fell
asleep that night.*

*Not too long thereafter, I was walking past the television one day
and heard the newscaster announce a recent bear rescue. In my heart of
hearts, I knew that this message was meant for me—that I was given
confirmation of how we truly can make a difference in any part of the*

world, no matter where we live. And yes, even when we're out eating popcorn and watching a movie.

Thank you, Dr. Joe and Dr. Hew Len and all of those before you who have brought the message of Ho'oponopono into our lives so that we can awaken and carry the knowledge that we have the power to heal the world and make a difference. Our work here has only just begun.

Please, let us always remember:

Harm none.

Love everything.

Love everyone.

Ho'oponopono travels across time. . . .

Suzanne Burns

www.ThankYouth.com

My Lifelong Search for an Asthma Cure Was Over . . .

One mysterious evening, after over 50 years of asthma and allergies, this condition abruptly, magically halted. Dateline: February 25, 2006.

Earlier that day, while relaxing over an Austin Tex-Mex lunch, I felt a quickening in my being. Oooooh, it felt very mysterious, like something was happening and I was somehow being worked on. A wave of love overwhelmed me and then I resumed lunch.

That evening in the hotel meeting room an electricity filled the air—an inexplicable pulsing of excitement. Dr. Hew Len, the speaker, ended up sitting at my table. Midway through the meal I told an asthma experience I had, and he used that later to springboard into his talk.

Well, I was familiar with the Hawaiian huna *spiritual healing model but not the healing and forgiveness methodology and philosophy at the heart of the healing, which he explained at length. Dr. Hew Len told us he was working on clearing each of us in attendance at the dinner, by reading our names and getting clarity and "oneness" with us.*

How he does it is by expressing love for each person, asking for forgiveness for any wrongdoing consciously or unconsciously from the past or present of himself and his ancestors, to us and our predecessors, all the way back to the beginning of time and microbic life forms. Wow! That's a lot to clear—so that he and we can all get back to true relationship in and of Divinity.

The next day unveiled the miracle at hand. I met my mentor (from Joe Vitale's Executive Mentoring Program) and his wife for lunch, being that I was from out of town and we'd never met in person. I had to walk quite a few blocks to the restaurant and realized I didn't need an inhaler at all during the trek. That was most unusual and the first clue. They remarked how far it was from where my car was parked and I told them that perhaps I no longer had asthma and that it felt like it was so.

Later that evening I had the pleasure of dining with Dr. Hew Len and we spoke of the healing of Ho'oponopono and that now, having experienced its power in my life with asthma, I could go and help others with this problem. He also spoke of the importance of drinking water before each meal to flush out toxins and also to rid the home environment of clutter. Ahem!

Well, the best got better and better. It's been nearly six months since, and even though I got bronchitis, I bounced back without medicines. I never wheezed or needed an inhaler or asthma drug of any sort. Since then I've been in homes with cats, dogs, and birds for hours at a time and had no wheezing or need for inhalers. My lungs are clear as a bell and I can breathe deeply and fully, and this for the first time ever. Wow!

Dr. Hew Len, though you don't call it a healing or yourself a healer, and would say that the universe and my soul did it, thank you, and thanks to Joe Vitale for sharing Dr. Hew Len and a night of healing magic! I'm forever grateful.

Martha Snee
www.translimits.com

And here's one more:

An Irishman Finds Aloha

Ten years ago, I began the study of myself through the use of Ho'oponopono. I came into the understanding of this Hawaiian problem solving process after years of study in Asian systems of healing, martial arts, and energy work.

I had been through what could be called the wringer in terms of my search for what could be understood as enlightenment, and being Irish, I am always looking for the proof of the pudding (meaning seeing results versus smokescreens of words). Being raised in South Boston, Massachusetts (a tough as nails, Irish working-class neighborhood where the sounds of gunfire and police sirens were like inner city birdcalls), chances of discovering metaphysical understandings of the universe didn't often come up. So, upon finding an opportunity to attend a free lecture, I jumped at the chance to check out this Hawaiian understanding of life.

What I found was very different. Many systems utilize and move energy (like moving pieces on a chessboard). Ho'oponopono, however, awakened me to how to erase the negative elements that manifest as problematic situations inside myself (thus removing the chess pieces altogether). I was intrigued, to say the least. Many of the concepts at the time flew over my head, as all of the ideas were new to me. But at the end of the lecture, I figured I would give the two free tools that were given out as a gift a chance and began to use them as much as I could during the day and throughout my massage practice to see if the proof of the pudding was in the eating.

In the past, I practiced Tui Na, a form of Chinese medical massage, and over time, my viewpoint began to shift in terms of my understanding of treatments. Before doing the tools, I had a set understanding of what was wrong within a person based on the Asian traditions of energy and meridians. But as I used the tools, I noticed that my understanding of the how or why changed and that it did not correspond with my prior training, as I would be treating areas that had no correlation to the reported issues of the clients coming in. As I did so, the client(s) would report almost instant results for varied issues. Needless to say, I began to wrestle with my understandings and started to see a bigger picture of this Hawaiian art form begin to unfold. The next spring, I attended a full training and began to truly apply the methods and practices.

One day I received a call from a former client whom I will call J, a practicing psychologist. She asked me to see a patient of hers whom she was very concerned about (I will call her F), who had a clinical diagnosis of bipolar disorder, attempted suicide numerous times, and was committed on a few occasions for her own safety. I said to J, "What did I ever do to you?" She laughed and said, "I know you can help her. You have to. If you don't, she won't make it." So I agreed. At the end of the call, J also said that F was once attacked by a massage therapist. I asked myself, "What am I going to do to help this woman?"

When I went home that evening, I sat for a while and wondered what could I do. How could I effect change on this level? After some introspection, Ho'oponopono! Ho'oponopono! kept playing in my mind like a broken record. So I began to use the tools as I never had before. I put marathon efforts into each session before, during, and well after, never telling F anything about my secret. During our meetings, the treatment room was full of humor and the air had a sense of thick peace to it as I cleaned. To make a long story short, F had a complete turnaround and is now a productive woman able to handle life as it comes. She is walking proof that if we take 100 percent responsibility, situations can indeed shift.

My massage practice also has shifted and has moved ahead, and I rarely touch anyone anymore. Currently, I find myself driving through life, hitting speed bumps now and then, amazed at where the cleaning will bring me next. Has it been simple? No, but I truly value all the situations that have come up and made me realize who I am.

After many years as a volunteer for the Foundation of I, Inc. Freedom of the Cosmos, my viewpoint is simple:

There will always be stuff coming up in one form or another, be it family issues, stress, opinions, or war, and in the beginning it was hard to accept that fact. Now instead of saying "Why me?" (inducing a guilt response), rather I say "I am responsible" (without guilt), and simply let go through the usage of the tools and let God take over.

It is a tough, tough job to do. *Did I say* tough? *But I have faith that a smoothness is occurring and that we just can't grasp the totality of it, because there are so many realities that coexist in the same time frame as ours. We should not waste time with the how, why, or when, rather just the "do."*

By doing so, we get out of the way of ourselves. As soon as we step outside of ourselves at all, in any manner, to blame, react, moan, groan, and so on, we lose sight of the issue at hand—namely, our chance to let go of the problem that is inside of us. If we blame, we become disconnected (like not paying our cable bill, zap! no HBO).

The choice for us is to not get all self-righteous, nor depressed, but simply to continue on without judgment against the most precious gift—the self.

If I slip up in the cleaning, I get up, brush myself off, and begin anew—one more chance to see the proof of the pudding.

Thank you.

Brian Om Collins

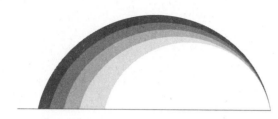

How to Create Faster Results

You don't say "Please forgive me" to the Divine because the Divine needs to hear it; you say it because you need to hear it.

—Dr. Ihaleakala Hew Len

D espite all the evidence you read in the preceding chapter, I still had my doubts. I told Dr. Hew Len that I couldn't always see immediate results from cleaning. He said, "If you could see the array of results from your cleansing and the cleansing of others, you would be awed. And you would do more cleansing. You hold the errors of the world in your soul, as well as I do in mine," he added. "Shakespeare is really incredible in his insight: 'Poor soul, the center of my sinful earth, / [Thrall to] these rebel pow'rs that thee array. . . .' [Sonnet 146]."

Shakespeare notes that reason (intellect) causes madness, confusion, unclarity:

> Past reason hunted; and no sooner had,
> Past reason hated, as a swallow'd bait,
> On purpose laid to make the taker mad . . .
>
> Sonnet 129

Shakespeare notes the problem of memories:

> When to the sessions of sweet silent thought
> I summon up remembrance of things past,
> I sigh the lack of many a thing I sought,
> And with old woes new wail my dear times' waste.
>
> . . .
>
> Then can I grieve at grievances foregone,
> And heavily from woe to woe tell o'er
> The sad account of fore-bemoanèd moan,
> Which I new pay as if not paid before.

Sonnet 30

Morrnah notes the purpose of the gift of life from the Divinity:

> Clean, erase, erase, and find your own Shangri-la. Where? Within yourself.

Shakespeare and Morrnah are messengers giving insights into the mystery of existence.

I was as open-minded as a person could get—at least a person named Joe Vitale, or even Ao Akua. But I still wasn't understanding the essence of what Dr. Hew Len was trying to tell me. But I hung in there. I remembered what I wrote in my earlier books: Confusion is that wonderful state before clarity.

Well, I was in that "wonderful state."

A lot of therapists come to Dr. Hew Len, complaining that they feel sick or feel like they can't help the people they see. I could relate. I started a miracles coaching program at www.miraclescoaching.com and wanted my coaches to understand that the way to heal others is by healing themselves; the others were in fact already perfect. Dr. Hew Len explained it in an e-mail like this:

> A student in the Self I-Dentity through Ho'oponopono class this past weekend in Calabasas, California, suddenly cried out loudly in the afternoon session as I was talking:

"My God. I now know why I feel sick in my stomach when I do healing with my clients. I've been deliberately taking on their woes. And I don't have to. I can clean the woes away."

The student got part of the insight that "healers" don't get. What they don't get is that the client is perfect. The client is not the problem. The healer is not the problem. The problem is what Shakespeare calls "old woes new wail my dear times' waste."

The problem is error memories replaying in the Subconscious, the Unihipili, that the "healer" shares in common with the client.

Self I-Dentity through Ho'oponopono is a problem solving process of repentance, forgiveness, and transmutation that anyone *can apply to themselves*. It is a process of petitioning Divinity to convert error memories in the Unihipili to zero, to nothing.

So it is with you. Error memories in your Unihipili are replaying problems, be it weight or your son or whatever. And the Conscious Mind, the Intellect, is clueless. It has no idea what is going on.

This being so, Ho'oponopono appeals to the Divinity within, who knows, to convert whatever memories are replaying in the Unihipili to zero.

A point needs to be made. Expectations and intentions do not have any impact on Divinity. Divinity will do whatever and whenever in its own way and time.

While I still wasn't understanding all of this yet, I did grasp the power of saying "I love you." It seemed innocent enough. What harm could come from saying "I love you" all the time? None. In fact, zero.

As Dr. Hew Len once explained, "To open the way for the in-flow of Divine wealth requires *first* canceling memories. As long as memories (blocks/limitations) are present in the Subconscious, they block Divinity from giving us *our daily bread*."

I began to feel that this whole "I love you" cleaning and clearing and erasing tool needed to be shared with the world. Since I'm enough of an entrepreneur to see a product here, I talked to one of my business partners, Pat O'Bryan, about making a special audio of the method. He quickly agreed. While he wrote the music, and I recorded the four phrases, I also wrote the web site copy. (You can find it at www.milagroresearchinstitute.com/iloveyou.htm.)

That web site and audio became a best seller for Pat and me. But what felt better than the sales was the fact that we were helping people awaken to the power of a simple cleaning process. Imagine the thought of thousands of people all saying "I love you"!

Mark Ryan—the friend who first told me about the mysterious therapist who helped heal mentally ill criminals—also joined me in creating a product based on Dr. Hew Len's insights.

Mark and I developed a subliminal DVD. The idea is to make change easy and effortless. All you do is slide the DVD into any player, sit back, and watch the show. What you hear are stories told by either Mark or myself, and original music. What you see consciously are beautiful settings, such as islands and clouds. What you don't see consciously are subliminal messages that flash on the screen for just moments. These messages are like telegrams to your unconscious. They flash the words needed to help you let go of any resentments so you can feel love. The entire DVD is designed to help someone forgive and love again. (See www.subliminalmanifestation.com.)

This product was designed to help people clean the negative blocks within themselves. As they cleaned, they got closer to experiencing the bliss of the zero limits state of being.

I was learning that ideas were coming to me as I continued to clean. I began to call this Inspired Marketing. In the past I might try to create a new product by combining existing ideas or products. Now I was finding it much more powerful, and less stressful, to simply allow ideas to come to me. All I had to do at that point was act on them. That's how Pat and I came up with the "I love you" recording. That's how Mark and I created the subliminal DVD. The ideas appeared in my mind and I acted on them.

If you stop and consider the implications of this, you might find yourself in awe. What I'm saying is that to just keep cleaning is far more important than anything else. As you clean, ideas are given to you. And some of them could make you very, very wealthy.

Dr. Hew Len offers several ways to do nonstop cleaning of his own creation. One of them is a symbol that came to him in an inspiration one day. This is it:

He put the symbol on his business card, and made stickers and buttons out of it. (See www.businessbyyou.com.) The word *Ceeport* means, he says, "Clean, Erase, Erase, while returning back to Port—the zero state."

Because I'm today convinced cleaning is the only way to get faster results, I wear *two* pins. I also place the symbol as a sticker on everything, from my cars to my computer to my wallet to my gym equipment. I'd stick it to my forehead if I didn't think it would look strange. Of course, I could always get it as a tattoo.

One day, when Dr. Hew Len came to visit me to discuss this book, I showed him my new business card. A friend had taken a picture of me standing in front of my latest new car, a 2005 Panoz Esperante GTLM, a hand-assembled exotic luxury sports car made outside of Atlanta. I knew I looked confident and probably radiated wealth in the picture but I had no idea just how powerful the image was. (See the photo of Francine and me on my business card.)

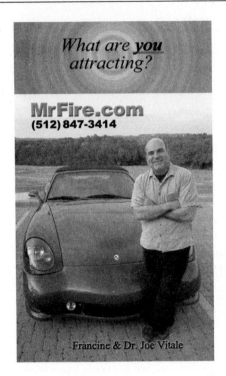

*What are **you** attracting?*

MrFire.com
(512) 847-3414

Francine & Dr. Joe Vitale

"This is a cleaning tool," Dr. Hew Len said after looking at it a few moments. "You can clean memories and negativity by swiping your business card over things, or people, or yourself."

Whether he's right or not, I sure felt better about my card and was more than willing to pass it out to people. I instantly waved the card over my body, to clean any negativity around me. Dr. Hew Len smiled and laughed.

Dr. Hew Len said the company logo for the Panoz car, an original crest with a yin-yang swirl and a three-leaf clover in it, was also a cleaning tool. He stared at the bright red, white, and blue colors and the green clover in it, and said it was a powerful symbol for cleaning, too. Since I love my Panoz and drive it a fair amount, thinking that it was cleaning me as I sat behind the wheel made me smile.

And the most beautiful thing about my business card is that it contains a picture of my car, with the Panoz crest right there on the hood. So the business card is a double whammy of a cleaning tool.

I'm sure it's talk like this that makes people think Dr. Hew Len is off his rocker. But whether you think he's crazy or not, the results I and others are getting with "crazy" cleaning tools like my business card or his Ceeport design are real. Listing them here won't make much of a difference, though, if your mind is purely skeptical. After all, hearing about people who stick Ceeport designs in their office to increase sales probably seems dumb or at best superstitious. Well, maybe it's the placebo effect: It works because you believe it works. If so, I say keep doing it.

Marvin, for example, a salesman who you'll read about in the next chapter, is breaking all records selling luxury cars to customers. He told me he sticks Ceeport stickers "everywhere."

"I stick them under my desk, on my ceiling, on my computer, on the coffee pot, under cars, in the showroom, in the waiting room, and more," he said. "I don't get a discount for buying these stickers, either. I buy hundreds and use them everywhere."

Maybe it's his belief in the cleaning tool that makes it work.

Or maybe the tool itself does all the work.

Who knows for sure?

A medical doctor once told me, "All medicine involves props and placebos."

If my business card is a placebo, it's a far less expensive one than many others.

I say if it works, do it.

Clean, clean, clean.

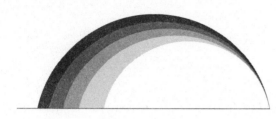

How to Receive Greater Wealth

I am the "I."

Owau no ka "I."

My next seminar with Dr. Hew Len was different from the first. While the message was still about cleaning and erasing programs or memories, his approach was even more relaxed and off-the-cuff. He began by holding up a baseball and asking what the point of the game was.

"To hit a home run," someone said.

"To win," said another.

"To keep your eye on the ball," I said.

"Exactly!" Dr. Hew Len responded, in his thick Hawaiian accent. "To win or hit a home run, you must keep your eye on the ball at all times. But what is the baseball in your life?"

Everyone was silent.

"Your breathing," someone said.

"This moment," someone else said.

Dr. Hew Len could see we weren't getting the point, so he offered an answer: "The baseball is Divinity," he said. "You must stay focused on going back to zero. No memories. No programs. Zero."

Cleaning. Cleaning. Cleaning.

All you're here to do is clean or not clean. You can choose all you like, but you don't decide if you get it or not. You trust Divinity to do what's right for you. Would you know better than Divinity? Hardly. Let go.

Clean. Clean. Clean.

"My intention is to be in alignment with the Divine's intention," I told Dr. Hew Len.

"Good for you, Joseph."

Intentions are limitations. You decide you want a front-row parking place. You intend it. But Divinity gives you a parking place a mile away. Why? Because you need to walk more. Let go.

Clean. Clean. Clean.

I spend two more days with Dr. Hew Len. Thirteen people are in the room. The whole focus is on how problems occur.

"You'll always have problems," he declares. I resist that statement but write it down anyway. Clean. Clean. Clean.

"Problems are memories replaying," he says. "Memories are programs. They aren't just yours. They are shared. The way to release the memory is to send love to the Divinity. Divinity hears and responds, but in the way best for all, at the time right for all. You choose but you don't decide. Divinity decides."

I didn't understand. Clean. Clean. Clean.

Marvin, a happy, broadly smiling fellow from the Philippines, gets up and explains that he sells $150 million worth of luxury cars a year by not trying to sell anything to anyone. All he does is clean.

"All I do is say 'I love you' all day long," he explains in his accented English. "I clean as I listen to people. All I do is clean, clean, clean. Always cleaning."

"You don't intend anything at all?" I asked, skeptical. I figure he's at least intending to sell cars, since that's his job.

"Never," he replies. "No expectations. I just show up to work and clean."

Clean. Clean. Clean.

I spent two days hearing stories about cleaning by average people like you and me. But it's all so hard to accept. Just clean and say "I love you" and the world changes? You sell more cars? You make more money? Huh?

"You are totally responsible for all of it," says Dr. Hew Len. "It's all in you. All of it. No exceptions. You have to clean on it or it doesn't get cleaned."

Clean on terrorism?

Clean. Clean. Clean.

Clean on the economy?

Clean. Clean. Clean.

Clean on—(fill in the blank)?

Clean. Clean. Clean.

"If it's in your experience, it's up to you to clean," says Dr. Hew Len.

When I take a break and call home to see how Nerissa and our pets are doing, Nerissa stuns me by saying she spent the day making a surprise for me. She had a long to-do list. Making anything for me didn't seem likely.

"What is it?" I ask.

"A major surprise."

"Tell me."

"You'll never guess in a million years," she says.

"Don't make me guess. I don't have a million years."

Before I tell you what she said, let me back up a second. Nerissa has been stressed because of so many projects on her plate. She can't keep up. She's working on a video for me, and another for a client. She created software she wants to promote. She also has the critters and the house to tend to while I'm away. She barely has time to plan her day, let alone work on her many projects. So imagine my surprise when she told me the following:

"I took apart your closet and rebuilt it."

Clean. Clean. Clean.

I'm stunned. Cleaning my closet was not on her to-do list or even on mine.

"I took down all your clothes, took down the shelves, built new shelves, rehung your clothes, put your piled-up clothes on hangers, and rearranged the clothes that were on the floor."

This is as shocking to me as if she had left a check for me made out for, say, five million dollars.

This was unbelievable.

"What made you do all this?" I asked.

"I've wanted to do it for a while now," she replied.

She wanted to do it? Maybe so. But she had no time. This came out of the blue.

Dr. Hew Len says when you clear memories, what comes through is inspiration. Nerissa was apparently inspired to clean my closet. It's a metaphor and proof that inner cleaning leads to outer results.

You can't intend what the outer results will be.

Again, you can choose but you can't decide.

Later, in Dr. Hew Len's motel room, he and I sit like master and disciple. The only thing is, he treats me like the master.

"Joseph, you are one of God's original 10."

"I am?"

I'm flattered but admit I have no idea what he is talking about.

"You came here to help awaken the Divine in people," he explains. "Your writing is hypnotic. It is your gift. But there's more."

"More?"

Clean. Clean. Clean.

"You are the J man for business," he says. "Do you know what that is?"

I don't have a clue and tell him so.

"You are the Jesus of business," he says, "the point man for change."

As he speaks, I'm thinking I'd better keep this conversation to myself. No one will ever believe it. I don't.

Clean. Clean. Clean.

"When I was with Morrnah," he says, reflecting on his years with the kahuna who taught him the updated form of Ho'opono-pono he teaches today, "I thought she was crazy for the first five years. But then one day that thought was gone."

Dr. Hew Len's style is rambling, poetic, and visionary. He seems to use the right and left sides of his brain at the same time, while the rest of us lean on one or the other side. He goes from telling me I'm the savior of business to telling me about Morrnah. In its own way, it's hypnotic. I'm riveted. I want more.

"There's a wreath around your head, Joseph," he says, seeing something I don't see or feel. "It's made of money symbols, like eagles."

For some reason I feel an urge to show him a ring I wear. It's a solid gold ring, 2,500 years old, from ancient Rome. He holds out his hand and I lay it on his palm.

"The word on the ring is Latin," I explain. "*Fidem* means faith."

Dr. Hew Len is silent as he holds the ring. He seems to be receiving images or impressions. I'm quiet while he seems to be tuning in to the ring itself.

"You were a great orator in a past life," he says. "But you were mobbed and murdered. This ring is healing that memory for you."

That's interesting. I often had flashes of being a legendary orator in the past, but I feared public speaking today because I was killed in the past after speaking. I thought it was an ego-designed memory, not a past life. Somehow Dr. Hew Len picked up on the memory by holding my ring.

"I rarely wear it," I confess.

"Wear it," he says. "Always."

He stares at the ring.

"This is amazing," he says. "This ring was worn by a healer who knew the value of 'Know thyself.'"

I'm fascinated. Dr. Hew Len has the aura of a calm sea in a storm of reality. While the world swirls about, he seems still. He speaks his heart, accepting whatever comes and whatever is said. He stares at me and looks at my feet.

"Joseph, my God, I should be sitting at your feet," he says, genuinely moved by whatever he sees in me. "You are as gods."

Clean. Clean. Clean.

"We're just here to clean," he reminds me and everyone else during our weekend training. "Clean always, incessantly, to clean all memories so Divine can inspire us to do what we came here to do."

Clean. Clean. Clean.

During the training I realize I had cleaned on one of my books and not on another. I had spent time loving *The Attractor Factor*, which became a number one best seller. But I didn't spend much time loving one of my other books, *There's a Customer Born Every Minute*, which didn't sell as well. I realize this with a bolt of energy up my spine. This is why it hadn't done as well as my other books.

When I attended the first training I learned I could use the eraser end of a pencil to help clean. I would tap the item with the eraser. That's it. It's a symbol if not a fact of cleaning memories. I set out a copy of my new book at the time, *Life's Missing Instruction Manual*, and put the pencil on it. Every day for months I tapped on it. Whenever I walked by it, I paused, picked up the pencil, and tapped the eraser end on the book. Call it nuts. But it was a psychological trigger to help me clean any memories surrounding the book. Well, that book became an instant best seller and stayed number one for four days. Major companies bought thousands of copies. Wal-Mart stocked it. *Woman's Day* magazine featured it.

But I hadn't done any cleaning on *There's a Customer Born Every Minute*. The book came out. It went close to the best-seller list but didn't hit the top 10. I also orchestrated a major publicity stunt to help bring attention to the book. It got some attention but no immediate sales. I told Dr. Hew Len about this.

"Dunk the book in your mind in a glass of water with fruit in it," he advised. "I know it's crazy. But mark today's date, dunk book in water, and see what happens."

He also surprised me by asking about Oprah.

"You want to go on her show?"

I stammered that I would love to at some point. At that time I hadn't yet been on the *Larry King Live* show, so Oprah's show seemed like quite a jump.

"You have to be clean so you don't choke," he advised.

Clean. Clean. Clean.

"Two authors went on and choked," he explained.

"I don't want that," I said.

"When you go on Oprah, it will be for her reasons, not yours," he said.

"That sounds profound," I commented.

"You have to give up the idea that people do things for you. They do things for themselves. All you have to do is clean."

Clean. Clean. Clean.

Before I left Dr. Hew Len on this trip, I again asked him about his years as staff psychologist at the hospital for the mentally ill criminals.

"I want you to be clear about something," he told me. "It wasn't easy and I didn't do it alone."

I left wanting to know more. Much more.

Clean. Clean. Clean.

It appears that everyone who does Ho'oponopono has a rather hypnotic story to tell. For example:

Dear Dr. Hew Len,

I attended the Ho'oponopono gathering in Philadelphia recently. I want to thank you deeply and humbly from a melting heart for reminding me of the way Home. I am eternally grateful to the Divine, to you, and to all the children who help you do this work of teaching.

What follows is a testimonial of sorts in response to the workshop. It is a sharing for those who might wonder about the power of Ho'oponopono. If it would be helpful to share, please do. If not of interest, discard and may my gratitude to all be sufficient.

Deep heartfelt thanks to you all.

May God grant you all peace, wisdom, health, and a long life in which to clean and come Home.

Much, much love and blessings,
Dana Hayne

Testimonial of Philadelphia Ho'oponopono Gathering

Dr. Hew Len began the workshop with a lecture and drawings. He laid out the cosmology of Ho'oponopono. He asked us, "Who are you? Do you know?" Together we explored the incredible, eternal, limitless, total, complete, empty, zero reality of our true Selves from which all peace emanates. "Home" he called it. We then explored with him the nature of "What is a problem?" "Have you ever noticed," he asked, "that wherever there is a problem, you are there? Does that tell you anything?" Like old Socrates, he engaged us in the process, coaxing questions and answers. Little did I know that Dr. Hew Len was deftly exhuming these hidden memories and judgments for cleaning and transformation.

Caught in the net, I raised my hand, asked questions, and made comments. However, as the days went by, it began to feel to me as though every time I asked Dr. Hew Len a question, he put me down. I felt "dissed." Each answer burned me and I felt publicly shamed and humiliated.

By Sunday morning, I was so angry with Dr. Hew Len I wanted to leave. I judged him as arrogant, controlling, and dominating. I sat there stewing, angry, ready to cry.

I was so angry, I wanted to leave. Unsure whether I was going to bail or not, I did get up and go to the bathroom, afraid I would start crying right there in the meeting room. I sat in one of those ammonia-filled stalls and felt the rage, which my anger had now become. Oh, I felt such murderous rage. Some part of me didn't want to let go of that rage. But something else kept prompting me to keep saying, "Forgive me. Forgive me. And I love you."

I kept saying this over and over to the rage. And then I realized that this was not a new feeling, that I had felt this same rage percolate and disguise itself as a slow burn in the background of my consciousness before—whenever my husband would put me down or whenever (and always) my lawyer mother had insisted on being right. And, oh, she was one whose words could make black look white, confusing the innocent heart of this child.

And then I understood. I "got it." Aha! This is it! This is some ancient memory, the beam in my eye, the beam I thrust into others' hearts. This is the sword of memory that I carry in my heart and drag into my "now" and slay others with—Dr. Hew Len, my mother, my husband, Bush, Saddam Hussein, whomever I can accuse and slay out there. This is what Dr. Hew Len is talking about, the continual loop of tape that keeps playing over and over again.

I did not leave. I went back into the conference room, and experienced a deep calm the rest of the day. I kept silently saying in my head, "I'm sorry. Please forgive me. Thank you. I love you." When Dr. Hew Len answered questions after that, I felt only love from him, none of the previous emotions. He hadn't changed at all. Something in me had.

Some time after I returned to the room, Dr. Hew Len shared a personal experience about his own introduction to Ho'oponopono. He had bailed the course, not once, but three times, each time thinking that the instructor was "crazy" and each time forfeiting the cost of the workshop. Did he know what I was thinking? Did he know that I had also almost just left because I thought he was crazy?

During the next break, I cautiously approached Dr. Hew Len. Very lovingly, he explained that the ancient, oft-repeated memory of male dominance had raised its head. He explained that this was a memory

*common to many and needed great persistence and diligence to heal. It
would not be until I returned home that I would begin to understand
the depth of healing that had occurred for me at the workshop.*

*Throughout the weekend, Dr. Hew Len gave us tools for
transformation, tools that totally defy intellectualism. Not expecting
results, I dutifully but skeptically held my pencil, said "Dewdrop," and
tapped the three words that I had written on a sheet of paper, words that
for me represented problems— "computer," "son," and "husband."
Again, I wouldn't know the power of these words until I got home.*

*When I got home, my husband and son greeted me. Both grinning,
they said, "Guess what we got while you were out." "A new
computer?" I guessed. We had been having computer problems, which
defied hours upon hours (no lie) of technical support from in-home
technicians to the point that I was seriously wondering if we had a
computer nasty, be it jinni or ghost. More importantly, we had been
having many family meltdowns in the past few weeks over our fickle
computers. I didn't care about computers. I just wanted harmony.*

*I was a little surprised when both spouse and son said yes, they had
bought a new computer. They had agreed just the previous night to wait
another six months to get one with the new 64-bit processor. They then
said, "Guess what kind." I went down the list: Dell, Hewlett-Packard,
Sony, Gateway, Compac, and so on. I named every kind of computer you
could think of. "No. No. No," they said to each guess. "I give up!" I cried.*

*Now, my husband of 30 years is a man of very strong ideas. He
has an iron will, which when focused and conscious is nothing less than
fantastic determination. When he's not so conscious, this determination,
however, can feel more like stubbornness and nothing can move him. He
had been a staunch PC advocate, and nothing, I mean nothing, would
have changed his mind. So when they both shouted at me, "Apple!"
you could have scraped me off the floor. You see, originally I had wanted
an Apple, but Apples were not allowed in our home any more than pork
is allowed in a kosher home.*

This might seem trivial to some. But I have been married for 30 years. And for 30 years, my marriage has traversed hills and valleys, the two of us struggling toward a mutual goal of unity and equality. This apparently inconsequential choice of computers represented a "laying down of the sword" that only those engaged in the battle would recognize. I mean if you had told me that China freed Tibet, I would not have been more surprised.

I remembered mentally lifting my pencil, saying "Dewdrop," and tapping "husband," "computer," and "son." Could 30 years of conflict be so quickly and effortlessly dissolved? Could saying "I'm sorry," "Forgive me," "Thank you," and "I love you" transform a lifetime of external conflicts with my authority figures—mother, phone company, and husband? All I know is that it's been two weeks since the workshop. I practice daily what Dr. Hew Len taught me as religiously as I can. My son's over a long, protracted illness, and my husband and I are dialoguing about things I used to keep bottled up and withheld. Oh, and last night he said, "You know, honey, if you'd like, you can get one of these little laptops for yourself."

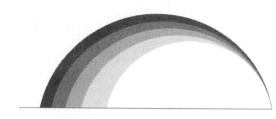

Skeptical Minds
Want to Know

*The purpose of life is to be restored back to Love, mo-
ment to moment. To fulfill this purpose, the individual
must acknowledge that he is 100 percent responsible for
creating his life the way it is. He must come to see that it
is his thoughts that create his life the way it is moment to
moment. The problems are not people, places, and situations but rather the thoughts of them. He must come to
appreciate that there is no such thing as "out there."*
                                    —Dr. Ihaleakala Hew Len

As I mentioned earlier in this book, I wrote an article called "The World's Most Unusual Therapist" and posted it on my blog. I added it to my web site at www.mrfire.com, as well. It was also published in a book by David Riklan, *101 Great Ways to Improve Your Life*. This article became the most widely distributed and talked-about article I had ever written. People posted it on newsgroups, forwarded it to friends, sent it to their personal and public e-mail lists, and more. Apparently the message in it was inspiring everyone. It was that very article that got the attention of my publisher, John Wiley & Sons, and led to my writing this book for you.

But not everyone loved the article. A few people couldn't believe that anyone, even a psychologist, could help heal mentally ill criminals in a hospital. One person wrote to Dr. Hew Len and demanded proof. The person wanted to know the facts about Dr. Hew Len's experiences in that mental hospital. So did

I, truth be known. Here's what Dr. Hew Len wrote as a detailed reply:

The story, as most stories go, needs clarification.

It is true that:

1. I spent several years as a fee-paid service staff psychologist at Hawaii State Hospital, a psychiatric facility operated by the Hawaii State Health Department.

2. I spent three years from 1984 to 1987 as the staff psychologist, 20 hours a week, in a high-security unit housing male patients who had committed criminal acts of murder, rape, drug use, and assault and battery against people and property.

3. When I entered the high-security unit in 1984 as the staff psychologist, all seclusion rooms were occupied with violent patients.

4. On any given day on the unit there were several patients in metal restraints around their ankles and wrists to prevent violence against others.

5. Violence in the unit by patients against patients and patients against staff was a common occurrence.

6. Patients were not intimately involved in their care and rehabilitation.

7. There were no in-unit rehabilitative work activities.

8. There were no off-unit activities, recreation, or work.

9. Visits by families on the unit were extremely rare.

10. No patients were allowed off of the high-security unit without written permission by the psychiatrist and only with ankle and wrist restraints.

11. The stay in the unit by a typical patient ran into years, the cost being, I believe, around $30,000 a year then.

12. Staff sick leave ran extremely high on the ward.

13. The physical environment of the unit was drab and somewhat rundown.

14. The unit staff was composed of basically wonderful and caring people.

15. What I've described is probably typical of most psychiatric units elsewhere in the country.

When I left the unit and facility in July 1987:

1. Seclusion rooms were no longer in use.

2. Wrist and ankle restraints were no longer in use.

3. Violent acts were extremely rare, usually involving new patients.

4. Patients were responsible for their own care, including arranging residential, work, and legal services before leaving the unit and the facility.

5. Off-unit recreational activities such as jogging and tennis were ongoing, not requiring approval by a psychiatrist or the use of ankle and wrist restraints.

6. Off-unit work activities were begun, such as car washing, without the approval of a psychiatrist or the use of ankle and wrist restraints.

7. On-unit work consisted of baking cookies and polishing shoes.

8. Visits in the unit by family were taking place.

9. Staff sick leave was not a chronic problem.

10. The unit environment greatly improved with painting and maintenance and because people cared.

11. The unit staff was more involved in supporting patients to be 100 percent responsible for themselves.

12. The turnaround time for patients from admission to leaving the hospital was greatly reduced to months instead of years.

13. The quality of life for both patients and staff shifted dramatically from being custodial to one of family, people caring for one another.

What did I do for my part as the unit staff psychologist? I did the Self Identity through Ho'oponopono process of repentance, forgiveness, and transmutation for whatever was going on in me that I experienced consciously and unconsciously as problems *before*, *during*, and *after* leaving the unit each time.

I did not do any therapy or counseling with patients on the unit.

I did not attend any staff conferences on patients.

I took 100 percent responsibility for myself to clean with the stuff in me that caused me problems as staff psychologist.

I am a creation of the I AM, perfect, as is with everyone and everything. What is imperfect is the c_ _p, the memories that react, replay as judgment, resentment, anger, irritation, and God knows the rest of the s_ _t that is carried in the Soul.

Peace of I,

Ihaleakala Hew Len, PhD, Chairman Emeritus

The Foundation of I, Inc. Freedom of the Cosmos

www.hooponopono.org

Though I was still learning ho'oponopono, I sometimes taught it to others if I felt they were open to hear about it. Of course, their being open was a reflection of me, not them. The clearer I became, the clearer the people around me became. But that's a tough fact to accept. It's so much easier to want to change the outer than the inner.

In Maui, a realtor drove us around to look at houses. Along the way, we did a lot of talking about healing, spirituality, the movie *The Secret*, and personal growth. It was all interesting, but something enlightening took place on one segment of our drive.

The realtor had read my now-famous article on Dr. Hew Len and the ho'oponopono Hawaiian healing process he used to heal an entire ward of mentally ill criminals.

Like everyone else, the realtor found the article inspiring.

Like everyone else, he didn't quite understand it.

As we drove around the beautiful island of Maui, I listened to the realtor complain about a house he couldn't sell. The buyer and seller were fighting over it, causing a lot of anger, resentment, and more. The sale was caught up in their bickering, and wasn't going to close anytime soon. The realtor was obviously frustrated by their actions.

I listened for a while and then felt inspired to speak up.

"Would you like to know how Dr. Hew Len might handle this situation using ho'oponopono?' I asked.

"Yes!" the realtor exclaimed, obviously curious. "I'm definitely interested. Tell me."

"This ought to be good," Nerissa said.

"Well, I'm not Dr. Hew Len," I began, "but I am writing a book with him and I've trained with him. So I think I know how he might handle this."

"Tell me!"

"What Dr. Hew Len does is look within himself to see what is within *him* that is sharing the experience he sees on the outside," I began. "When he worked at that mental hospital, he looked at the patients' charts. Whether he felt repulsion at their acts or something else, he didn't deal with the person; he dealt with the feelings *he* experienced. As he cleared what was within him, *they* began to get clear and heal."

"I like this," the realtor said.

"Most people have no idea what responsibility means," I continued.

"They are into blame. As they grow and become more aware, they begin to consider that they are responsible for what they say and do. Beyond that, as you become even more aware, you can begin to realize that you are responsible for what *everyone* says or does, simply because they are in your experience. If you create your own reality, then you created all you see, even the parts you don't like."

The realtor was smiling, nodding his head.

I kept talking.

"It doesn't matter what the buyer or seller does in this situation," I said. "It matters what *you* do. What Dr. Hew Len does is simply repeat 'I love you,' 'I'm sorry,' 'Please forgive me,' and 'Thank you.' He doesn't say it to the people, he says it to the Divine. The idea is to clear the shared energy."

"I'll do this," the realtor said.

"But you don't do it to get something," I went on. "You do it because it's how we clear the shared energy so no one has to experience it again, ever. It's a cleansing, and you never stop doing it."

I paused.

The realtor seemed to get it. His eyes were wide and his smile was big.

"If it comes up in your awareness," I continued, "then it's up for you to clean and heal. Since you brought this situation of the buyer and seller to *my* attention, then I have to clean on it, too. It's now part of my life experience. If I'm the creator of my experience, then this is something I'm responsible for, too."

I let all of this sink in as we continued our drive to look at other homes in Maui.

A few days later I received an e-mail from the realtor. He said he was continuing to use the Dr. Hew Len process.

That's how it works.

It's all love.

It's continuous.

And you're totally responsible.

One day I taught a seminar with Mindy Hurt, who runs the Wimberley, Texas, Unity Church. It was called "The Secret of Money." Later in it, I taught everyone the ho'oponopono method of cleaning. Afterward one gentleman came up and said, "I have a problem saying 'I'm sorry' and 'Please forgive me.'"

"Why?" I asked.

I had never heard this before. I was curious.

"I can't imagine a loving God or Divinity who needs my asking for forgiveness," he said. "I don't think the Divine has to forgive me for anything."

I thought about it and later knew the reply I should have given him:

"You aren't saying those statements to be forgiven by the Divinity; you're saying them to clean yourself. You say them *to* Divinity but they are to clean *you*."

In other words, the Divine is already showering love on you. It has never stopped. At the zero state, where there are zero limits, the closest we can describe it is as a state of pure love. It's there. But you're not. So by saying, "I love you, I'm sorry, please forgive me, thank you," you are cleaning the programs *in you* that are preventing you being at the pure state: love.

Again, the Divine doesn't need you to do ho'oponopono; but *you* need to do it.

Recently I received a heart-wrenching e-mail from a dear friend of mine. She asked:

"What would you say to someone who has been reading your book, who watched *The Secret*, who reads your blog every day, who does her best, yet is still broke, unhappy, and failing? I keep having problem after problem. It never ends. What would you say?"

I felt her pain. After all, at one point I was homeless. I struggled in poverty for a decade. My "overnight" success probably took 20 years to occur. I know what it's like to feel like you're stuck in quicksand.

What would you say to such a person?

In the past I would offer solutions. I would say read *The Magic of Believing* by Claude Bristol. Watch the movie *The Secret* seven times. Create a scenario of how you want life to be. Take time every day to meditate. Work on self-sabotage issues.

But that's the frontal approach to change. I've learned—and Dr. Hew Len will attest—that that approach rarely works.

So what's left?

How do you or me or anyone help someone stuck and in pain?

According to ho'oponopono, the only way is by cleaning myself. People who come before me—including the one who wrote me— are sharing a program with me. They caught it like a virus of the mind. They aren't to blame. They feel trapped or cornered. I can throw them a rope, but more often than not, they won't use it, or they'll use it to hang themselves.

So what do you do?

All I can do is clean *me*. As I clean me, they get cleaned. As we clean the programs we share, they get lifted from all humankind. This is all I do these days. It's what Dr. Hew Len first told me he did, on that first phone call we had so long ago: "All I do is clean, clean, clean."

All I do is say, "I love you," "I'm sorry," "Please forgive me," and "Thank you." The rest is up to Divinity. I don't think this is heartless but instead the most heartfelt thing I can do. And it's what I'm doing right now, even as I write these words.

Finally, consider this spiritual punchline:

Since the story of this person who wrote me is now part of your experience, that means it is up for you to heal, as well. After all, if you create your own reality, then you had to create *this* situation, too, as it is now part of your reality. I suggest you use the "I love you" statements to heal this.

As you heal yourself, the person who wrote me, and everyone else who shares that program, will get better.

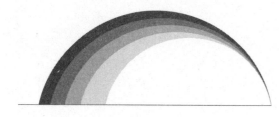

Choice Is a Limitation

We can appeal to Divinity who knows our personal blueprint, for healing of all thoughts and memories that are holding us back at this time.

—Morrnah Simeona

D r. Hew Len flew to Austin, Texas, to spend a few days with me in October 2006. When I picked him up at the airport, we instantly began talking about life, God, programs, cleaning, and more. He asked what I was up to these days. I told him how excited I am.

"There's a movie where a character says, 'Some people are awake, and they live in a constant state of amazement.' I am pretty close to that state," I said. "I have magic and miracles and feel exhilarated by life."

"Tell me more," he urged.

I told him about my new car, which I adore. It's a 2005 Panoz Esperante GTLM luxury exotic sports car. They are made by the Panoz family. Each is assembled by hand, each is signed by the people who make it, and each is given a name. My car is named Francine. I knew Dr. Hew Len would appreciate the love put into the car, and the fact that it is treated like a living person. For him, everything is alive.

I told him about going on the *Larry King Live* television show as a result of my being in the movie *The Secret*. He wanted to know what Larry King was like. I told him. King is direct, friendly, street-smart. I liked him.

I went on and told Dr. Hew Len about the success of my books, such as *The Attractor Factor* and *Life's Missing Instruction Manual*. After a few minutes he could see that I was just bubbling over with energy.

"What do you think is different now from you taking the first ho'oponopono training?"

I thought for a moment and said, "I quit controlling it all. I let go. All I do is clean, erase, and have the intention to get to zero."

He patted my shoulder and smiled, in a way anchoring the moment by acknowledging what he felt was right for me.

We started walking to my car, and after a few feet he stopped and stared at me.

"You have a bounce in your step," he said, almost in awe. "You walk with springs."

"Well, I *am* happy to see you," I said.

We went to dinner and I told him I was disappointed that my book on P. T. Barnum, *There's a Customer Born Every Minute*, wasn't doing well.

"Joseph, you have to love it."

I wanted my book to sell, so I didn't understand what love had to do with it.

"Joseph, if you had three children and one of them was slow in school, would you tell it that you were disappointed in it?"

"No," I replied. And suddenly an insight hit me hard. My book is a child of me, and I was saying it wasn't as good as my other children. I felt this to such a real degree that I almost began to cry in the restaurant.

"You got it, Joseph," Dr. Hew Len said. "You must love all your children."

I began to feel terrible that I had alienated my "child" for not performing well in the school of life. I felt genuinely sorry. I began to say "I love you," "I'm sorry," "Please forgive me," and "Thank you" in my mind to the Divine, while holding a sense of my book in my heart. Later, when I got home and saw my book, I picked it up and held it to my heart, hugging it, loving it, asking for forgiveness for not appreciating it just for being.

Later, driving Dr. Hew Len to my home area in Wimberley, Texas, he said he saw an elf in me.

"A what?"

"An elf," he repeated.

I'm used to him seeing things that I don't see. He wouldn't call it psychic ability but just an unfolding in each moment.

"The elf has big eyes and big ears. He wants to stay inside and not go out in public."

"That's the part of me that wants to stay at home and work on my computer and not interact with people."

"There's another part of you that likes the limelight, though."

"Two-thirds of me wants to be on *Larry King* and *Oprah* and get the attention," I confessed, "but another part wants to stay indoors and be reclusive."

"Your elf will keep you sane," Dr. Hew Len explained. "People who want nothing but stardom will drive themselves crazy. People who want nothing but living in a cave keep their light under a bushel basket. You have balance."

Later that day, I told Nerissa, my love, about my elf.

"What is the part of you called that likes to be onstage?" she asked.

"I don't know."

She reflected for a moment and said, "I think it's called Sprite."

"Sprite?"

"Yes, Sprite. It seems to fit."

I laughed and had to agree. The next day, when I told Dr. Hew Len that Nerissa named my extrovert part Sprite, he laughed out loud and loved it.

"Sprite likes the light," he sang.

The day after Dr. Hew Len arrived to my area, I drove over to meet with him. I found him sitting at a table with two retired Mexican women who seemed to be hanging on his every word. He motioned for me to come over. I got some coffee and started to sit in the chair beside him. He stopped me and asked me to sit in the next chair, one more chair away from him, but across from the two ladies.

"Tell these ladies what you do," he said to me.

I told them about my books, my movie appearance, and how I try to help people find happiness.

"Tell them how you handle problems," he said.

"In the past I used to try to solve problems, whether my own or someone else's. Today I let them be, but I clean the memories that caused them. As I do, they get resolved and I'm okay as they get resolved."

"Joseph, can you give them an example?"

"My sister frustrates me," I confessed. "She's been on welfare, had her home broken into, had her identity stolen, and more. She's not happy and it frustrates me. I've tried to help by sending her money, books, movies, and even the DVD player to play the movies. She doesn't make any effort to change. But now I don't try to change her."

"What do you do?" one of the ladies asked.

"I work on *me*," I said. "Now I understand that the life she has isn't anything she is doing. It's a program, or memory, that is being played and she's got in its web. It's like she caught a virus. It isn't her fault at all. And because I sense it, because I feel her pain, it means I share the same program. I have to clean. As I clean, the program will come off her, too."

"What do you do to clean?"

"All I do is say 'I love you,' 'I'm sorry,' 'Please forgive me,' and 'Thank you' over and over again."

Dr. Hew Len explained that in the simple phrase "I love you" are three elements that can transform anything. He said they are gratitude, reverence, and transmutation. I went on to explain what I thought was happening.

"The phrases I say are like the magic words that open the combination lock to the universe. When I recite the phrases, which come out like a poem, I am opening myself to the Divine cleaning me and erasing all the programs preventing me from being here now."

Dr. Hew Len said he liked how I described the ho'oponopono method of clearing.

"Saying someone caught a virus is accurate," he said. "It's a program that is in the world and we catch it. When someone has it and you notice it, then you have it, too. The idea is to take 100 percent responsibility. When you clean yourself, you clean the program from everyone." He paused and added, "But there are a lot of programs. They are like weeds on zero. To get at zero limits, we have more cleaning to do than you could ever imagine."

The ladies seemed to understand, which surprised me. We were talking about mind-bending concepts, yet they seemed to relate to them. I couldn't help but wonder if they were simply tuning in to Dr. Hew Len's vibe, much like a tuning fork sets a tone for everything around it that can feel its note.

Dr. Hew Len and I went for a walk. It was a half-mile stroll in the cool morning air on a dusty gravel road. Along the way deer walked around us. At one point we came across a group of dogs barking their heads off at us, but we kept talking and walking. Suddenly Dr. Hew Len waved his hand at them, as if to bless them, and said, "We love you."

The dogs stopped barking.

"All any of us want is to be loved," he said. "You, me, even the dogs."

One small dog behind the others gave out a slight yip. I couldn't stop thinking he was saying, "Right on" or maybe "Thank you."

Or even, "I love you, too."

Our conversations were always stimulating. At one point Dr. Hew Len blew my head off by explaining that the only choice in life is to clean or not.

"You're coming from either memory or inspiration," he explained. "That's it."

I replied, "I've always told people that they have the choice to come from inspiration or not. That's free will. The Divine sends a message and you can act on it or not. If you do, all is well. If you don't, you may have problems."

"Your choice is to clean or not," he said. "If you are clear, then when inspiration comes, you just act. You don't think about it. If you think about it, then you are comparing the inspiration to something, and what you are comparing it to is a memory. Clean the memory and you don't have choice. You just have inspiration and you act on it without thinking. It just is."

Whew! That insight truly shook me. I felt bad that I've been writing and speaking about choice being free will and now I learn that free will means you are still stuck in memory. When you are at the zero state and there are zero limits, you don't do anything but what is there for you to do. That's it.

"It's like we are in a grand symphony," Dr. Hew Len explained. "Each of us has an instrument to play. I have one, too. Your readers have theirs. None are the same. In order for the concert to play and everyone to enjoy it, they need to play their part and not another's. We get into trouble when we don't pick up our instrument or we think someone has a better one. That's memory."

I began to see that a concert has stagehands, promoters, and cleaning crew. Everyone has a role.

I also reflected on the different people I knew who seemed clueless to their own method of success. There's James Caan, the famous actor from *The Godfather* and the TV series *Las Vegas*. I've met him several times. His stardom is as much a mystery to him as it is to you or me. He's a brilliant actor, even legendary. But all he's do-ing is being himself. He's playing his part in the universe's script.

The same could be said for me. Some people who meet me act like I'm some sort of guru. If they've seen me in the movie *The Secret* or read any of my books, especially *The Attractor Factor*, they think I'm plugged into God's hotline. The truth is, I'm just playing my instru-ment in the concert of life.

When you play your role and I play my role, the world works. It's when you try to be me or I try to be you that problems arise.

"Who set up all these roles?" I asked Dr. Hew Len.

"Divinity," he said. "Zero."

"When was it set up?"

"Long before you and I ever showed up as even an amoeba."

"Does that mean there is no free will at all? That we're just stuck in our roles?"

"You have total free will," he said. "You're creating as you are breathing, but to live from zero you must let go of all memories to be there."

I have to admit I didn't fully understand all of this. But the part I did get was that it's my job to play my instrument. If I play mine, then I am a piece of the puzzle of life that found its slot. But if I try to fit myself into another area of the board, I won't fit, and the entire picture will be off.

"Your conscious mind will try to understand it all," Dr. Hew Len clarified. "But your conscious mind is aware of only 15 bits of infor-mation while there are 15 million bits happening all the time. Your conscious mind doesn't have a clue what's really happening."

That wasn't very comforting.

At least not to my conscious mind.

As I mentioned earlier, I taught a seminar one day called "The Secret of Money." I told everyone that they will have money if they are clear. If they are broke, they aren't clear. I told Dr. Hew Len about it and he agreed.

"Memories can keep money away," he said. "If you are clear about money, you'll have it. The universe gives it if you will accept it. It is memories playing that keep it from you or you from seeing it."

"How do you get clear?"

"Keep saying 'I love you.'"

"Do you say it to money?"

"You can love money but it's better to just say it to the Divine. When you are at zero, you have zero limits and even money can come to you. But when you are in memory, you will prevent it. There are many memories around money. As you clean them, they get cleaned for everyone."

We went into a deli and ordered coffee. The place was quiet as we sat there, but slowly people streamed in and the place got busier and louder. The energy in the place grew.

"You notice that?" he asked.

"There's a buzz to the place," I said. "People seem happier."

"We came in and we brought our cleaner selves and the place is feeling it," he said.

He told me about going into restaurants in Europe. Their business would be slow but after he visited, business increased. He tried this in a few different places to see if the same thing happened. It did. He then went to a restaurant owner and said, "If we come in and your business improves, will you give us a free meal?" The owner agreed. Dr. Hew Len would often get free meals from just being.

I noticed that he gave money freely. We went into a little shop. He bought a few stained glass items for friends. He then slapped a $20 bill on the counter and said, "And this is for you!" The clerk looked surprised and naturally so. He added, "It's only money!"

Later, at a restaurant, I gave a large tip to the waitress. She stared, openmouthed. "I couldn't accept this," she said. "Yes, you can," I countered.

Still, later, I got an idea for a product that I knew would make me a large amount of money. Dr. Hew Len pointed out, "The universe rewarded you for your generosity. You gave so it gave back. It gave you that inspiration. Had you not given, it would not have given."

Ah, and there was the real secret to money.

"We Americans forget that it says right on our money, 'In God We Trust,'" said Dr. Hew Len. "We print it but we don't believe it."

At one point Dr. Hew Len asked me about the nutritional company I had founded with a physician and a nutritionist. We created it to market a cholesterol-lowering natural formula we call Cardio Secret. (See www.CardioSecret.com.) Dr. Hew Len had consulted with me a while back about the product name as well as the name of the company. He was curious to see where we went with it.

"It's on hold right now," I said. "I hired a Food and Drug Administration (FDA) attorney to review our web site and our packaging, and we're waiting on him. But as a result of working on this product, I got an idea for an even more exciting product, something I call Fit-A-Rita."

I went on to explain that Fit-A-Rita is a natural margarita mix. (See www.fitarita.com.) I received the idea for it while out drinking with friends. I was in yet another bodybuilding fitness contest at the time, so having a margarita was a rare and special thing for me. While drinking one, I said, "What we need is a Bodybuilder's Margarita." As soon as I said it, I knew it was a good idea.

"Good for you, Joseph," Dr. Hew Len said. "You weren't attached to the first product and wanting things to go your way, so the Divine gave you a new moneymaking idea. Too many people lock onto an idea and try to force it to fit their expectations, and what they're doing is blocking the very wealth they want to receive. Good for you, Joseph, good for you."

He's right, of course. As long as I stay open to ideas from the Divine, they keep coming. Besides the Fit-A-Rita product, I also received an idea for "clearing mats." These are mats you place your food on to clean it and you before you dine. (See www.clearingmats.com.) But I didn't stop there. Dr. Hew Len received an idea, too.

"I've never seen a web site that cleans people while they sit and look at it," he told me. "Let's make our web site for our book just that. When people go there, they are being cleaned by what we infuse in the site."

We did just that, too. See it at www.zerolimits.info.

There's no end to the amount of ideas and money you can receive once you let go of your need and allow it all to come to you. The key, as always, is to just keep cleaning, cleaning, cleaning.

"What should therapists do when they see clients?" I asked, wanting to probe for specific methods in helping people to heal.

"Just love them," Dr. Hew Len replied.

"But what if someone comes to you because they were traumatized at some point and they aren't over it?" I asked, wanting to back Dr. Hew Len into a corner and force him to squeeze out some method I could use.

"All everyone wants is to be loved," he said. "Isn't that what you want? It doesn't matter what you say or do as long as you love the person."

"So I could be a Jungian or a Freudian or a Reichian or anything else?"

"It doesn't matter," he stressed. "What matters is that you love the person because they are a part of you, and your loving them will help erase and clean and clear the program activated in their life."

I wasn't settling for that answer, though I could see his point.

"But what if someone is certifiably crazy?"

"I had a woman come to me who was considered schizophrenic," he began. "I asked her to tell me her story. You have to understand that whatever she or anyone tells me isn't the real issue. Their story is their conscious interpretation of events. What's really happening is out of their awareness. But hearing the story is the starting place."

"What did she say?"

"She told me her story and I listened. I just kept repeating 'I love you' in my mind, to the Divine, trusting whatever needed to be cleaned would be cleaned. At one point she told me her full name, which was one of those hyphenated names."

"Like Vitale-Oden or some such?"

"Exactly. I knew that was part of the problem. When someone has a split name, it creates a split personality. She needed to own her birth name."

"Did you ask her to legally change her name?"

"She didn't have to go that far," he explained. "By telling herself that her name was one word, she began to relax and feel whole again."

"But was it the name change or your saying 'I love you' that made the difference for her?"

"Who knows?"

"But I want to know," I said. "I started a Miracles Coaching program at www.miraclescoaching.com. I want to be sure my coaches say and do the right thing so they truly help people."

He went on to explain that therapists think they are here to help people or save people. But in reality their job is to heal themselves of the program they see in their patients. As those memories get canceled in the therapist, they get canceled in the patient.

"It doesn't matter what you or your coaches say or do as long as they keep loving the person they are with," he explained again. "Remember, the person you see is the mirror of you. What they experience is shared by you. Clean the shared program and you'll both get well."

"But how?"

"I love you," he said.

I'm beginning to sense a theme here.

I've been trying to figure out how the world works since I was old enough to read children's books and then comic books. "Superman" and "The Flash" were pretty easy to understand. Today I have to deal with science, religion, psychology, and philosophy as well as my own mental wanderings.

Just when I think I have a handle on things, along comes another book to disturb my view of the world. This time I was reading *Consciousness Speaks* by Balsekar when I started to get a headache.

If I had to sum up its message in words from a man confused by reading the book, I'd say that nothing we do comes from free will. It's all being prompted through us. We think we are the conscious actors. We're wrong. That's our egos talking. In some respect, we're puppets with the Divine as the energy in us pulling our strings.

Now imagine this:

I'm the guy who wrote *The Attractor Factor*, a book that explains a five-step process for having, doing, or being anything you want. I and others have used the method to attract everything from wealth to cars to spouses to health to jobs to, well, you name it. It's all about declaring your intention and then acting on what comes your way or bubbles up from within to make it manifest. In short, you're the puppeteer and the world is your puppet.

So how do I fit these two apparently conflicting philosophies in my head without going bonkers?

I think it works like this:

First, we are living in a belief-driven world. Whatever you believe, that belief will work. It'll get you through the day, at any rate. It will frame your experiences into perceptions that make sense to you. And when something comes your way that doesn't seem to match your worldview/belief system, you'll find a way to rationalize it and force it to fit. Or you'll take valium.

Second, I can't help but wonder if both philosophies are right: We're the puppet and the puppeteer. But that only works when we get out of our own way. It's our minds that drive us to overdrink, overeat, frolic, steal, lie, and even spend too much time worrying about how the world works. Our minds get in the way of the natural flow of things. Our minds know they are doomed and they can't stand the thought of it, so they construct feel-good addictions to help them survive. In reality (whatever *that* is), your mind is the interference to experiencing the bliss of this moment.

If this is so, then all the techniques to get clear—which I talk about as step three in *The Attractor Factor*—are there to help you take the *interference* out of the Divine plan.

For example, when you use a method like the Emotional Freedom Technique (EFT)—the tapping your troubles away approach to life—you dissolve the issues troubling you.

But then what happens?

Then you take a positive action.

Well, weren't you going to take that positive action anyway?

Isn't that why you knew there was a problem to begin with?

In other words, the nudge to take action was sent to you from the Divine, and your anxiety over it was the interference. Take away the interference and you're back to being one with the Divine, which means you're puppet and puppeteer again.

So let me try to sum up what at least makes sense to me today:

You came into this world with a gift within yourself. You may know it right away or not. You may not even know it right now. At some point you'll sense it within you. Now, your mind is going to judge it. If your mind judges it as bad, you'll seek therapy or methods or drugs or addictions to handle it, hide it, resolve it, release it, or accept it. But once you have removed that interference preventing you from acting on your gift, you'll act on that gift. In short, you'll be the puppet of the Divine but you'll be the puppeteer of your life.

Your choice is to go with the flow or not.

That's free will. Some call it "free won't" because your real decision is to act on the impulse or not.

Even the great showman and marketer P. T. Barnum, whom I

wrote about in my book *There's a Customer Born Every Minute*, knew this. He took action. He did things on a grand scale. But he was always obeying some higher order. His gravestone marker reads, "Not my will but thine be done."

He acted on his ideas without interference from his mind, and he allowed the results to be what they were, trusting that it was all part of the universe's bigger picture. He was able to let go *while* taking action.

And that's step five in my book, *The Attractor Factor*.

Tonight I have the world figured out. (I think.)

Tomorrow I'm not so sure.

I long for comic books again.

"Everyone has a gift," Dr. Hew Len told me on one of our walks.

"What about Tiger Woods?" I asked, knowing the answer but wanting to lead to a deeper question.

"He's playing his role in the Divine play."

"But what about when he starts to teach others how to play golf?"

"He'll never succeed," Dr. Hew Len said. "His role is playing golf, not teaching golf. That's someone else's role. We each have our part."

"Even a janitor?"

"Yes! There are janitors and garbage collectors who love their work," he said. "You don't think so because you are imagining playing their roles. But they can't play your role, either."

I suddenly remembered a line from an old self-improvement course: "If God told you what to do, you'd do it and be happy. Well, what you are doing is what God wants you to do."

The point is not to resist your role. I might long to be a songwriter like Michelle Malone, or an actor like James Caan, or a bodybuilder like Frank Zane, or a writer like Jack London. I might even get pretty good at writing songs, or acting, or working out, or writing novels. But *my* role is *inspirator*. I write books to awaken people, or to be exact, to awaken *me*.

As I awaken me, I awaken you.

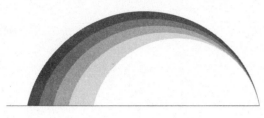

Cigars, Hamburgers, and Killing the Divine

Cleaning helps reduce the mortgage on your soul.
                    —Dr. Ihaleakala Hew Len

One day Dr. Hew Len wanted to get something to eat. It was on a Monday evening. We were in my small town, where everybody is busy entertaining tourists on the weekend and often closes on Monday to recover. There was only one place open that I could think of, a hamburger joint called Burger Barn. I didn't want to even mention the place, as I figured Dr. Hew Len would not want un-healthy food. Plus with my lifestyle change and new eating habits, I didn't dare even drive near a fast-food place. But I told Dr. Hew Len about it, anyway.

"A burger sounds great!" he said, obviously excited.

"Are you sure?" I asked.

"Oh, yeah! I love a good burger."

We drove to the place and parked. We went in and sat. The menu didn't have much on it of a healthy food choice nature.

"I'll have a double meat, double cheese burger on a white bun," Dr. Hew Len ordered.

I was stunned. That was heart attack food, in my opinion. Meat? Cheese? And a white bun? I couldn't believe it. I also couldn't believe that I ordered the same thing. I figured if it was good enough for the shaman it ought to be good enough for me.

"Aren't you worried about the cheese and meat and bread?" I asked him.

"Not at all," he said. "I have a chili dog every morning for break-fast. I love this stuff."

"You do?"

"It's not the food that is dangerous," he explained to me. "It's what you think about the food."

I had heard that comment before, but I never believed it. I fig-ured the solid trumped the thought. But maybe I was wrong.

He went on to explain, "Before I eat anything, in my mind I say to the food, 'I love you! I love you! If I am bringing anything into this situation that would cause me to feel ill as I am eating you, it's not you! It's not even me! It's something that triggers that I am will-ing to be responsible for!' I then go on and enjoy the meal, because now it's clean."

Once again his insights startled me and awakened me. I had spent so much time reading about health issues and food warnings that I was so paranoid I couldn't enjoy a simple hamburger. I decided to clean on it. When the food arrived, we ate it with gusto.

"This hamburger is the best I've ever had," he announced. He was so impressed that he went and asked for the cook, and then thanked him. The cook wasn't used to people acknowledging his deep-fried burgers. He didn't know what to say.

Neither did I.

When I gave Dr. Hew Len a tour of my home, including my gym, I held my breath. I keep cigars in my gym. It seems ironic to work out in the morning and smoke in the evening, but there you go; that's my life. But I worried that Dr. Hew Len might say something about my smoking.

I showed him my various types of equipment, pictures of famous bodybuilders on the walls, and the certificates I've received for the fitness contests I've been in. I tried to steer him away from the cigars sitting on a bench. But he noticed them.

"What's this?" he asked.

"Cigars," I said with a sigh.

"You smoke working out?"

"No, no, but I do in the evening," I explained. "It's my meditation time. I sit on the deck, smoke, and feel gratitude for my life."

He was silent for a moment. I was waiting for him to rattle off all the statistics showing why smoking is bad for you. Finally, he spoke.

"I think it's beautiful."

"You do?" I asked.

"I think you should smoke a cigar with your Panoz car."

"What do you mean? Have a picture taken of me in front of Francine with a cigar in my hand?"

"Maybe, but I was thinking you can smoke while you polish her or dust her down."

"I thought you were going to ridicule me for smoking," I finally told him. "One person read my blog, saw I mentioned cigars, and wrote me that I was putting toxins into my body and hurting myself."

"I guess that person never heard of the American Indian custom of passing the peace pipe," he said, "or how smoking in many tribes is a rite of passage and a way to bond and share and be a family."

I was once again learning that the key for Dr. Hew Len is to love everything. When you do, that thing changes. Smoking is bad when you think it is bad; hamburgers are bad when you think they are bad. As with everything in the ancient Hawaiian traditions, it all begins with thought, and the great healer is love.

I was finally beginning to understand him, and how important it is to get to the zero limits state.

But not everyone felt the same as me.

One night I went on a teleseminar and told everyone about my experiences with Dr. Hew Len, most of which I've told you here. They listened attentively. They asked questions. They seemed to understand what I was explaining. But to my surprise, at the end of the call they resumed their normal way of thinking. While all agreed that we need to take 100 percent responsibility for our lives, they were again talking about others. While all agreed that the cleaning method Dr. Hew Len taught me was powerful, they again went back to old habits.

One person said, "I don't want to say 'I'm sorry,' because whatever I say after 'I am' is what I will become."

I wanted to say, "Well, we can clean on that," knowing that her statement was just a belief. But I simply said, "Dr. Hew Len says do whatever works for you."

I admit at first I found this frustrating. But then I realized *I* had to clean on this, too. After all, if I take 100 percent responsibility for what I experience, I am experiencing *them*. And if the only tool with which to clean is "I love you," then I need to clean on what I see in others, as what I see in others is *in me*.

This may be the hardest part of ho'oponopono to understand. There's nothing out there. It's all in you. Whatever you experience, you experience inside yourself.

One person challenged me on this issue by asking, "What about the 50 million people who voted for the president I don't like? Clearly I had nothing to do with their actions!"

"Where do you experience those 50 million people?" I asked.

"What do you mean where do I experience them?" he countered. "I read about them, I see them on television, and it's a fact they voted for him."

"But where do you experience all of that information?"

"In my head, as news."

"Inside yourself, right?" I asked.

"Well, I process the information inside myself, yes, but *they* are outside of me. I don't have 50 million people in me."

"Actually, you do," I said. "You experience them in you, so they don't exist unless you look within yourself."

"But I can look out and see them."

"You see them inside yourself," I stated. "Everything you process is in you. If you don't process it, it doesn't exist."

"Is this like if a tree falls in a forest and no one is there, does it make a sound?"

"Exactly."

"This is crazy."

"Exactly," I said. "But it's the way home."

I then decided to test him even further. I asked, "Can you tell me what your next thought will be?"

He was quiet for a moment. He wanted to blurt out an answer but realized he couldn't.

"No one can predict their next thought," I explained. "You can verbalize it once it occurs to you, but the thought itself arises from your unconscious. You have no control over it. The only choice you have is once the thought appears, to act on it or not."

"I don't follow."

"You can do any number of things once the thought arises, but it's being generated in your unconscious," I explained. "In order to clean the unconscious so you get better thoughts, you have to do something else."

"Such as?"

"Well, I'm writing a whole book about it," I replied, referring to this book you're reading.

"And what does this have to do with the 50 million people out there?"

"They're no more out there than your own thoughts are," I said. "It's all inside you. All you can do is clean in order to clear out the storehouse of programs in your mind. As you clean, the thoughts that arise get more positive and productive and even loving."

"I still think all of this is batty," he said.

"I'll clean on that," I replied.

Most likely he never got it. But if I'm to get to zero limits, I have to take total responsibility for him not getting it. His memory is my memory. His program is my program. The very fact that he voiced it to me means I share it with him. So, as I get clear of it, so will he. As I'm writing this, I'm saying "I love you" in my thoughts, behind the words, behind the typing, behind the computer, behind the scenes. My saying "I love you" as I work, write, read, play, talk, or think is my attempt to do nonstop cleaning, erasing, and clearing of anything and everything between me and zero.

Can you feel the love?

One morning Dr. Hew Len said he saw a logo for me containing a four-leaf clover. "The fourth pedal is gold, like a tongue," he said. He spent several minutes describing what he was seeing in his mind, or in the air. I'm not sure where he was getting his impression. Neither was he.

"You need to find an artist to sketch the logo for you," he said.

Later we went for a walk into town. We had lunch and then visited a few shops. The first shop contained stained glass art. We were both impressed. As we admired the shopkeeper's handiwork, she said, "If you ever need a logo or a sketch, we can draw it for you."

Dr. Hew Len grinned and leaned in my direction, as I grinned and leaned in his. Coming from zero meant synchronicity happened.

While I was writing this section of the book, I had to stop to be interviewed for another movie. This one is like *The Secret* but focused on getting healthy with your thoughts. I began the interview by saying thoughts weren't as important as no thoughts. I tried to explain the zero limits state of being, where you allow the Divine to heal you, not you heal yourself. I wasn't sure why I was saying all this. A part of me questioned my sanity. But I went with the flow.

After the camera was turned off, the woman observing it all almost blurted out that she heals people by entering the zero state. It turned out she is a physician who now heals animals by entering the no-thought zero limits state of being while in the presence of the ill animals. She showed me pictures of dogs with cataracts, and then the after photos where they are completely healed.

Once again, the Divine was proving that the Divine has all the power, not me. I can just clean so I can hear it and obey it.

Last night I spent an hour and a half on the phone with a best-selling author and self-help guru. I've been a fan of his for years. I love all his books. I'm a groupie for his message. Since he also likes my work, we finally connected and talked. But I was stunned by what we talked about.

This personal growth expert narrated a horrifying true story of his last couple of years. He had been victimized and abused by someone he loved. While I listened, I wondered how he could say he was a victim when his published message was about taking responsibility for your life.

It began to dawn on me that almost everyone—even the self-help experts who try to teach us how to live (including me)—don't have a clue what they are doing. They are still missing a piece of the puzzle. They get to a point where they think what worked in the past for them will work at all times in the future, and for everyone else. But life isn't like that. We're all different and life is always changing. Just when you think you have it figured out, along comes a new wrench and your life looks out of hand once again.

Dr. Hew Len's work teaches us to let go and trust the Divine while constantly cleaning all the thoughts and experiences that surface in the way of hearing the Divine. By this continuous work, we can clear the weeds of programs so we can better handle life with ease and grace.

As I listened to the self-help author narrate his journey of woes, I kept saying "I love you" quietly, inside my mind, to the Divine. By the time he was done talking, he seemed lighter and happier.

As Dr. Hew Len keeps reminding me and everyone else, "The Divine is not a concierge. You don't ask for things; you just clean."

I loved spending time with Dr. Hew Len. He never seemed to mind my questions. One day I asked him if there were any advanced methods for cleaning. After all, he has been doing ho'oponopono for more than 25 years. Surely he's created or received some other methods besides "I love you" to clear memories.

"What do you do these days to clean?" I asked.

He chuckled and said, "Kill the Divine."

I was stunned.

"Kill the Divine?" I repeated, wondering what he meant.

"I know that even inspiration is one step removed from the zero state," he explained. "I'm told that I have to kill the Divine to be home."

"But how do you kill the Divine?"

"Keep cleaning," he said.

Always, always, always, it kept coming back to the one singular refrain that healed any and all wounds: "I love you, I'm sorry, please forgive me, thank you."

When I was in Warsaw, Poland, at the end of 2006, I decided to introduce the idea of zero limits and the zero state to my audience. I had been there speaking for two days about hypnotic marketing and my book, *The Attractor Factor*. I found the people to be open-minded, loving, and eager to learn. So I taught them what I've shared with you here: that you are responsible for everything in your life and that the way to heal everything is with a simple "I love you."

Though the audience needed a translator for my presentation, they seemed to absorb my every word. But one person asked me an interesting question:

"People here in Poland spend all day praying to God and going to church, yet we have had war, our city was bombed by Hitler, we lived under martial law for years, and we have suffered. Why didn't those prayers work, and what's different with this Hawaiian one?"

I paused to consider the right answer, wishing Dr. Hew Len was here to help me. In the moment I gave this reply:

"People don't get what they say so much as what they feel. Most people who pray don't believe they will be heard or they will be helped. Most people pray from a place of desperation, which means they will attract more of what they are feeling: more desperation."

My questioner seemed to understand and accept my answer. He nodded. But when I returned to the United States, I wrote Dr. Hew Len and asked him what he would have replied. He wrote back the following e-mail:

Ao Akua:

Thank you for the opportunity to clean with whatever is going on in me that I experience as your question.

An American showed up in the class that I did in Valencia, Spain, two years ago. "My grandson was ill with cancer," she said to me in a break. "I prayed for him, asking that he not die, but he died anyway. How come?"

"You prayed for the wrong person," I said. "Better to have prayed for yourself, asking forgiveness for whatever was going on in you that you experienced as your grandson being ill."

People don't see themselves as the source of their experiences. Rarely are prayers directed at what is going on in the petitioner by the petitioner.

Peace of I,

Ihaleakala

I loved his perfectly honest answer. Again and again, his theme is that nothing is outside of us. When most people pray, they act like they have no power or responsibility. But in ho'oponopono, you are totally responsible. The "prayer" is to ask for forgiveness for whatever is in you that caused the outer circumstance. The prayer is a reconnecting to the Divine. The rest is trusting the Divine to heal you. As you heal, so does the outer. Everything, without exception, is inside you.

Larry Dossey said it well in his book, *Healing Words*: "We need to recall at these times that prayer, in its function as a bridge to the Absolute, *has no failure rate*. It works 100 percent of the time—unless we prevent this realization by remaining oblivious to it."

One thing bothered me about my work with Dr. Hew Len.

As I kept growing and having insights, I worried that all my previous books were wrong and were going to mislead people. In *The Attractor Factor*, for example, I praised the power of intention. Now, years after writing that book, I knew intention is a fool's game, an ego's toy, and that the real source of power is inspiration. I also now knew that agreeing to life is the great secret to happiness, not controlling life. Too many people, myself included, were visualizing and affirming in order to manipulate the world. I now knew that isn't necessary. You're better off going with the flow while constantly cleaning whatever comes up.

I began to feel like Neville Goddard must have felt. Neville is one of my favorite mystical writers. His early books were about creating your own reality by turning "feeling into fact." He called it "the law" in such books as *The Law and the Promise*. "The law" referred to your ability to influence the world with feeling. "The promise" referred to surrendering to God's will for you.

Neville began his career by teaching people how to get what they want with what he called "awakened imagination." The short description of that phrase refers to Neville's favorite quote, "Imagining creates reality." His very first book was titled *At Your Command*, which I later updated. In it he explained that the world is indeed "at your command." Tell the Divine or God what you want, and it will be delivered. But by Neville's later years, after 1959, he had awakened to a greater power: that of letting go and letting the Divine operate *through* you.

The thing is, he couldn't recall his earlier books like a car manufacturer might recall a defective car. I have no idea if they upset him or not. I'm guessing not. He left them in the world because he felt "the law" was useful to help people get through the bumps in life. But I wanted to recall my books. I felt they were misleading people. I told Dr. Hew Len that I felt like I was doing a disservice to the world.

"Your books are like stepping-stones," Dr. Hew Len explained. "People are at various steps along the path. Your books speak to them where they are. As they use that book to grow, they become ready for the next book. You don't need to recall any books at all. They are all perfect."

As I thought of my books, of Neville, of Dr. Hew Len, and of all the readers past, present, and to come, all I could say was, "I'm sorry, please forgive me, thank you, I love you."

Clean. Clean. Clean.

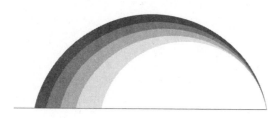

The Truth
Behind
the Story

It's not your fault but it is your responsibility.

—Dr. Joe Vitale

I wasn't done with Dr. Hew Len. I still didn't have the complete story on his work at that mental hospital.

"You never saw patients?" I asked him again one day. "*Never?*"

"I saw them in the hallway but never as a patient in my office," he said. "One time I saw one of them and he said, 'I could kill you, you know.' I replied, 'I bet you could do a good job, too.' "

Dr. Hew Len went on to say, "When I started at the state hospital working with the criminally mentally ill, we had three or four major attacks between patients every day. There were maybe 30 patients at that time. People were shackled, put in seclusion, or restricted to the ward. Doctors and nurses walked through the halls with their backs against the walls, afraid of being attacked. After just a few months of cleaning, we saw a complete change for the better: no more shackles, no more seclusion, and people were allowed to leave and do things like work and play sports."

But what did he do, exactly, to begin this transformation?

"I had to take complete responsibility within myself for actualizing the problems outside myself," he said. "I had to clean my own toxic thoughts and replace them with love. There wasn't anything wrong with the patients. The errors were in me."

As Dr. Hew Len explained it, the patients and even the ward didn't feel love. So he loved everything.

"I looked at the walls and saw they needed to be painted," he told me. "But none of the new paint would stick. It would peel off right away. So I simply told the walls that I love them. Then one day someone decided to paint the walls and this time the paint stuck."

That sounded weird, to say the least, but I was getting accustomed to this sort of talk from him. I finally had to ask the question that had been bothering me the most.

"Did *all* of the patients get released?"

"Two of them never were," he said. "They were both transferred elsewhere. Otherwise, the entire ward was healed."

Then he added something that truly helped me understand the power of what he had been doing.

"If you want to know what it was like during those years, write Omaka-O-Kala Hamaguchi. She worked as the social worker during the time I was there."

I did. She wrote the following to me:

Dear Joe,

Thank you for this opportunity.

Please know that I am writing this in collaboration with Emory Lance Oliveira, who is a social worker who worked on the unit with Dr. Hew Len.

I found myself the social worker assigned to the newly opened forensic unit at the state mental hospital in Hawaii. This unit was called the Closed Intensive Security Unit (CISU). It housed prisoner-patients who had committed often heinous felony crimes of murder, rape, assault, robbery, molestation, and combinations thereof, and were also diagnosed with or thought to possibly have a serious mental disorder.

Some of the prisoner-patients had been found not guilty by reason of insanity (NGRI) and sentenced to be there; some were floridly psychotic and required treatment, and some were there for examination and assessment to determine their fitness to proceed (i.e., their ability to understand the charges against them and participate in their own defense). Some were schizophrenic, some bipolar, and some mentally retarded, while others were diagnosed psychopaths or sociopaths. There were also those who were trying to convince the courts they were one or all of the above.

All were locked in the unit 24/7 and allowed to leave escorted in wrist and ankle restraints only for medical or court appointments. Most of their day was spent in a seclusion room, a locked room with concrete walls and ceilings, a locked bathroom, and no windows. Many were highly medicated. Activities were few and far between.

"Incidents" were expected occurrences—patients attacking staff, patients attacking other patients, patients attacking themselves, patients attempting escapes. Staffing "incidents" were also a problem—staff manipulating patients; drugs, sick leave, and workers' compensation problems; staff discord; perpetual turnover in psychologist, psychiatrist, and administrator positions; plumbing and electrical problems; and so on and so on. It was an intense, volatile, depressing, and wild place to be. Even the plants would not grow.

And even when it was relocated to a newly renovated, much more secure unit with a fenced recreation area, no one expected anything to really change.

So when "another one of those psychologists" showed up, it was assumed he would try to stir things up, attempt to implement state-of-the-art programs, then leave almost as soon as he came—ho hum.

However, this time it was a Dr. Hew Len, who, besides being friendly enough, appeared to do next to nothing. He didn't do evaluations, assessments, or diagnoses; he provided no therapy and did not perform any psychological testing. He often came late, and did not *attend case conferences or participate in mandated record keeping. He instead practiced a "weird" process of Self I-Dentity Ho'oponopono (SIH), which had something to do with taking 100 percent responsibility for yourself, looking only at yourself, and allowing the removal of negative and unwanted energies within you—ho hum.*

Weirdest of all was the observation that this psychologist seemed always at ease and even to be really enjoying himself! He laughed a lot, had fun with patients and staff, and seemed to genuinely enjoy what he was doing. Everyone seemed to love and enjoy him in return, even if it didn't appear he did much work.

And things began to shift. Seclusion rooms began clearing; patients were becoming responsible for their own needs and business; they also began participating in planning and implementing programs and projects for themselves. Medication levels were also dropping and patients were being allowed to leave the unit sans restraints.

The unit became alive—calmer, lighter, safer, cleaner, more active, fun, and productive. The plants began to grow, plumbing problems became almost nonexistent, incidents of violence on the unit became rare, and staff seemed more harmonious, relaxed, and enthusiastic. Rather than sick-leave problems and understaffing, overstaffing and losing positions now became a concern.

Two specific situations made an especially memorable impact on me.

There was a severely delusional, paranoid patient with a history of violence who had seriously hurt several people in the hospital and out in public, and who had had multiple hospital admissions. He was sent to CISU this time for committing a murder. He was creepily frightening to me. The hairs on the back of my neck stood up whenever he was anywhere close.

It was, then, much to my surprise that a year or two after Dr. Hew Len showed up, I spotted him walking in my direction escorted sans restraints and the hairs on the back of my neck did not stand up. It felt as if I was just noticing, without judgment, even when we passed each other almost shoulder to shoulder. There was not my usual getting-

ready-to-run reaction. In fact, I noticed he looked calm. I was no longer working on the unit at that time but had *to find out what had happened. I learned he had been out of seclusion and restraints for some time and the only explanation was that some of the staff were doing the ho'oponopono Dr. Hew Len had shared with them.*

The other situation occurred while I was watching the news on television. I had taken a mental health day off to get away from work and relax. The court appearance of a CISU patient who had molested and murdered a three- or four-year-old girl showed up on the news. This patient had been hospitalized as he was deemed unfit to proceed on the charges against him. He was examined and evaluated by several psychiatrists and psychologists and given an array of diagnoses which, back then, would have most likely gotten him a not guilty by reason of insanity (NGRI) judgment. He would not have had to go to prison and would have been committed to the less restrictive setting of the state hospital with the possibility of a conditional release.

Dr. Hew Len had interacted with this patient, who eventually asked to be taught the SIH process and reportedly was very persistent and consistent in its practice, like the ex-marine officer he was. He, by now, had been deemed fit to proceed and had a court date to state his plea.

Whereas most other patients and their attorneys had opted and would probably always opt for the NGRI plea, this patient did not. The day before he was to appear in court he dismissed his attorney. The following afternoon, he stood in court facing the judge and regretfully and humbly proclaimed, "I am responsible and I am sorry." No one expected this. It took a few moments before the judge could grasp what had just happened.

I had played tennis with Dr. Hew Len and this fellow on two or three occasions and, though the patient was most polite and considerate, I had judgments. However, at that very moment, I only felt tenderness and love for him and sensed a huge shift in the entire courtroom as

*well. The judge and attorneys' voices were now gentle, and all those
around him seemed to be looking at him with tender smiles. It was a
moment.*

*So when Dr. Hew Len asked if some of us would like to learn
about this ho'oponopono after tennis one afternoon, I jumped fast and
high, anxiously waiting for the tennis game to come and go. It's now
almost 20 years later and I am still awed by what I have since learned
was the Divinity working through Dr. Hew Len at Hawaii State
Hospital. I am eternally grateful to Dr. Hew Len and the "weird"
process he brought with him.*

*By the way, in case you're wondering, this patient was found just
plain guilty and was in a sense rewarded by the judge, who granted his
request to serve his sentence in a federal penitentiary in his home state
where he could be near his wife and children.*

*Also, though almost 20 years have passed, I received a call this
morning from the former secretary of the unit wanting to know if Dr.
Hew Len would be available anytime soon to get together with some of
the old staff, most of whom have since retired. We will be meeting with
them in a couple of weeks. Who knows what may unfold? I'll keep my
antennae up for further stories.*

Peace,
O.H.

And there it was. Dr. Hew Len had indeed accomplished a miracle at the hospital. By practicing love and forgiveness, he transformed people who were hopeless and in many ways considered throwaways of society.

That's the power of love.

I wanted to know even more, of course.

As I was completing the first draft of this book, I sent it to Dr. Hew Len for review. I wanted him to check it for accuracy. I also wanted him to fill in any holes in the story about his years at that mental hospital. About one week after he received the manuscript, he wrote the following e-mail to me:

Ao Akua:

This is a confidential note to you and to you alone. It comes from my reading the draft of *Zero Limits*. I have other comments to make on the draft but I will leave them for later e-mails.

"You're done," Morrnah said without being emphatic.

"I'm done with what?" I replied.

"You're done with Hawaii State Hospital."

Although I sensed the finality of her comment that summer day in July 1987, I said, "I have to give them two weeks' notice." Of course I didn't. It never came up to do so. And no one from the hospital made mention of it.

I never returned to the hospital even when I was invited to attend my farewell party. My friends had it without me. The farewell gifts were delivered to the Foundation of I office following the party.

I loved my stay at Hawaii State Hospital in the forensic unit. I loved the folks on the ward. At some point, I don't know when, I passed from being staff psychologist to being a member of the family.

I lived closely with staff, patients, rules, polices, cliques, and forces seen and unseen on the ward for three years, 20 hours a week.

I was there when seclusion rooms, metal restraints, medication, and other forms of control were regular and acceptable modes of operation.

I was there when the use of seclusion rooms and metal restraints simply evaporated at some point. When? Nobody knows.

Physical and verbal violence evaporated, too, almost completely.

The drop in medication use occurred on its own.

At some point, who knows when, patients left the unit for recreation and work activities without restraints and without needing medical approval.

The transformation of the ward from being crazy and tense to being peaceful simply occurred without conscious effort.

The transformation of the ward from being chronically understaffed to being "overstaffed" simply took place.

So, I want to make it clear that I was a close and active family member on the ward. I was not an onlooker.

Yes, I provided no therapy. I did no psychological testing. I attended no staff meetings. I did not participate in case conferences on patients. I did, however, become intimately involved in the workings of the ward.

I was present when the first in-ward work project—baking cookies for sale—appeared. I was present when the first off-ward activity—car washing—appeared. I was present when the first off-ward recreation program started.

I didn't carry out the usual functions of a staff psychologist not because I felt that they were useless. I just didn't do them for whatever unknown reasons.

I did, however, walk the ward and took part in the baking of cookies and in jogging and tennis games off-ward.

But more than anything, I did my cleansing before, during, and after each visit to the ward week in and week out for three years. I cleaned with whatever was going on in me with the ward every morning and every evening and if anything about the ward came up in my mind.

Thank you.

I love you.

Peace of I,

Ihaleakala

I loved this further clarification. While it revealed a humbleness on Dr. Hew Len's part, it also helped explain what he did and did not do while employed at the hospital.

I wrote him back and asked for his permission to include the e-mail here, to share it with you. He wrote back one word—the one I expected him to write: "Yes."

I'm not done with what I can learn from this amazing man. We decided we would begin to lead seminars together and of course be co-authors of this book. But at least now I had the complete story on how he helped heal an entire ward of mentally ill criminals. He did it like he does everything: by working on himself. And the way he works on himself is with three simple words: "I love you."

This is the same process you and I can do, too, of course. If I had to sum up the modernized Self I-Dentity through Ho'oponopono method that Dr. Hew Len teaches in a few short steps, it might look like this:

1.   Continuously clean.
2.   Take action on ideas and opportunities that come your way.
3.   Continuously clean.

That's it. It may be the shortest route to success ever created. It might be the path of least resistance. It might be the most direct route to the zero state. And it all begins and ends with one magical phrase: "I love you."

That's the way to enter the zone of *zero limits*.

And yes, *I love you.*

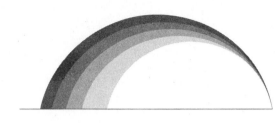

Epilogue

The Three Stages of Awakening

My job here on earth is twofold. My job is first of all to make amends. My second job is to awaken people who might be asleep. Almost everyone is asleep! **The only way I can awaken them is to work on myself.**

—Dr. Ihaleakala Hew Len

The other day a reporter asked me, "Where do you see yourself a year from now?"

In the past I would have given him a sincere accounting of what I hoped to achieve. I'd talk about my plans, goals, and intentions. I'd tell him about books I wanted to write or things I wanted to be, do, create, or buy. But because of all the work I've done with Dr. Hew Len, I no longer state goals or intentions or make plans for the future. So I instead replied with the truth of this moment:

"Wherever I'll be will be far better than what I can imagine right now."

There's more depth to that answer than you might first notice. It came from inspiration. The answer surprised me as I said it. It also revealed where my mind is these days: I'm more interested in *this* moment than the next one. As I pay attention to this moment, all the future ones unfold quite nicely. As I once told Dr. Hew Len, "My intention these days is to honor the intention of the Divine."

I relayed the reporter's question and my inspired answer to a friend just a few minutes ago. He loved it. He's been doing ho'oponopono with me for a few months now, so he understood the ultimate truth: When you let go of your ego and the ego's desires, you allow something better to guide you: the Divine.

This new me, and new understanding, is all part of my vivification. This didn't all happen overnight, of course. But by saying "I love you" and the other statements, I've been led to a deeper awareness, what some might call an awakening, maybe even enlightenment itself. I came to understand there are at least three stages to this awakening, and they're almost a map of life's spiritual journey. They are:

1. *You're a victim.* We are virtually all born feeling we are powerless. Most of us stay that way. We think the world is out to get us: the government, the neighbors, the society, the bad guys in whatever form they seem to take. We don't feel we have any influence. We're the effect of the rest of the world's cause. We gripe, complain, protest, and gather in groups to fight those in charge of us. Except for a party now and then, life, in general, sucks.

2. *You're in control.* At some point you see a life-changing movie, like *The Secret*, or you read a book, such as *The Attractor Factor* or *The Magic of Believing*, and you wake up to your own power. You realize the power of setting intentions. You realize the power you have to visualize what you want, take action, and achieve it. You begin to experience some magic. You start to experience some cool results. Life, in general, begins to look pretty good.

3. *You're awakening.* At some point after stage two, you begin to realize your intentions are limitations. You begin to see that with all your newfound power, you're still not able to control everything. You begin to realize that when you surrender to a greater power, miracles tend to happen. You begin to let go, and trust. You begin to practice, moment by moment, awareness of your connection with the Divine. You learn to

recognize inspiration when it comes to you, and you act on it. You realize you have choice but not control of your life. You realize the greatest thing you can do is agree to each moment. In this stage, miracles happen, and they constantly astonish you as they do. You live, in general, in a constant state of amazement, wonder, and gratitude.

I've entered the third stage, and maybe you have, too, by now. Since you've come along for the ride with me, let me try to further explain my own awakening. It may help prepare you for what you will soon experience, or help you better understand what you are currently experiencing.

I had a glimpse of the Divine in the first seminar with Dr. Hew Len. It was during those first days with him that I stopped my mental chatter. I accepted all. There was a peace almost beyond understanding. Love was my mantra. It was the song always playing in my brain.

But this glimpse didn't stop there.

Whenever I was in the presence of Dr. Hew Len, I felt peace. I'm sure it was the tuning-fork effect. His tone affected mine. It brought me into harmony with peace.

During the second seminar I began to have what some would call psychic flashes. I saw auras. I saw angels around people. I received images. I still remember seeing invisible cats around Nerissa's neck. When I told her, she smiled. Whether the image was real or not, it sure altered her mood. She beamed.

Dr. Hew Len often sees question marks floating above people's heads, which tell him which person to call on in an event. Whenever he sees invisible symbols or beings, he adds, "I know it sounds crazy. Psychiatrists would lock someone up for saying things like that."

He's right, of course, but once an awakening takes place, there's no looking back. In my first Beyond Manifestation weekend, I read some of the people's energy fields. They were in awe. I can't say this is a gift so much as it is an opening. A previously unused part of my brain turned on and lit up. Now my eyes see, if I let them. I told Dr. Hew Len, "Everything seems to talk to me. Everything seems alive." He smiled knowingly.

By the time of my second Beyond Manifestation weekend, I had another satori experience. Satori is a glimpse of enlightenment, a taste of the Divine. It's as though a window slides opens and for a moment you merge with the source of life. It's as difficult to explain as describing a flower from another planet. But by seeing that I could disappear and experience zero limits transformed me. I have that experience as a touchstone. I can recall it and return to it. On one level this is wonderful, as it's my ticket back to bliss. But on another level this is just another memory, keeping me from experiencing this moment. All I can do is keep cleaning.

Sometimes when I'm in a meeting, I'll relax and unfocus my eyes, and I'll be able to see the truth behind a situation. It's as though time stops or at least slows down. What I then perceive is the underlying tapestry of life. It's a little like peeling off the top level of a painting to find a masterpiece under it. Call it psychic vision, X-ray vision, or Divine sight. I'd say that "Joe Vitale" (and even "Ao Akua") disappears into the zero state, or my eyes perceive it. There are zero limits. There just *is*. At that place, there's no confusion. It's all clarity.

I don't live in that state. I still come back to so-called reality. I still have challenges. When Larry King asked me if I had a bad day, I said yes. I still do. Dr. Hew Len said we would always have problems. But ho'oponopono is a problem-solving technique. As long as I keep saying "I love you" to the Divine and I keep cleaning, I return to the place of zero limits.

The signal from zero is, if we try to put words on it, "love." So saying "I love you" nonstop helps us tune in. Repeating it helps neutralize the memories, programs, beliefs, and limitations that are in the way of your own awakening. As I keep cleaning, I keep tuning in to pure inspiration. As I act on that inspiration, better miracles than I could have ever imagined take place. All I have to do is keep at it.

Some people think they understand the voice of inspiration by paying attention to the tone of the voices they hear in their heads. A friend once said, "I know the difference between my ego's voice and inspiration's voice because the ego has an urgency to it and inspiration is gentler."

I think this is deceiving. A voice that sounds harsh and a voice that sounds gentle are still voices from the ego. Even right now, as you read these words, you are talking to yourself. You are questioning what you are reading. You've come to identify with that voice and to think it's you. It's not. Divinity, and inspiration, are *behind* those voices. As you keep practicing ho'oponopono, you keep getting clearer about what is actually inspiration and what isn't.

As Dr. Hew Len keeps reminding us, "This is not a fast-food approach to healing. It takes time."

I'd add that awakening can happen at any time. Even while reading this book. Or taking a walk. Or petting a dog. The situation doesn't matter. Your internal state does. And it all begins, and ends, with one beautiful phrase:

"I love you."

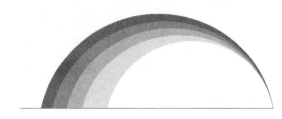

APPENDIX A

Zero Limits
Basic Principles

The Peace for always, now and forever and ever-more.

Ka Maluhia no na wa a pau, no ke'ia wa a mau a mau loa aku.

1. **You don't have a clue what is going on.**

   It is impossible to be aware of *everything* happening in and around you, consciously or unconsciously. Your body and mind are regulating themselves right now, without you being aware of it. And numerous invisible signals are in the air, from radio waves to thought forms, which you have no conscious sense of at all. You are indeed co-creating your own reality right now, but it is happening *unconsciously*, without your conscious knowledge or control. This is why you can think positive thoughts all you like and still be broke. Your conscious mind isn't the creator.

2. **You don't have control over everything.**

   Obviously, if you don't know everything that is happening, you can't control it all. It's an ego trip to think you can make the world do your bidding. Since your ego can't see much of what is going on in the world right now, letting your ego decide what is best for you isn't wise. You have choice, but you don't have control. You can use your conscious mind to

begin to choose what you would prefer to experience, but
you have to let go of whether you manifest it or not, or how,
or when. Surrender is key.

3. **You can heal whatever comes your way.**

Whatever appears in your life, no matter how it got
there, is up for healing simply because it's now on your radar.
The assumption here is that if you can feel it, you can heal it.
If you can see it in someone else, and it bothers you, then it's
up for healing. Or as I'm told Oprah once said, "If you can
spot it, you've got it." You may have no idea why it's in your
life or how it got there, but you can let it go because you're
now aware of it. The more you heal what comes up, the
clearer you are to manifest what you prefer, because you will
be freeing stuck energy to use for other matters.

4. **You are 100 percent responsible for all you experience.**

What happens in your life is not your fault, but it is your
responsibility. The concept of personal responsibility goes
beyond what you say, do, and think. It includes what *others*
say, do, and think that shows up in your life. If you take complete responsibility for all that appears in your life, then
when someone surfaces with a problem, then it is your
problem, too. This ties in to principle three, which states you
can heal whatever comes your way. In short, you can't blame
anyone or anything for your current reality. All you can do is
take responsibility for it, which means accept it, own it, and
love it. The more you heal what comes up, the more you get
in tune with the source.

5. **Your ticket to zero limits is saying the phrase "I love
    you."**

The pass that gets you peace beyond all understanding,
from healing to manifestation, is the simple phrase "I love
you." Saying it to the Divine cleans everything in you so you

can experience the miracle of this moment: zero limits. The idea is to love everything. Love the extra fat, the addiction, the problem child or neighbor or spouse; love it all. Love transmutes the stuck energy and frees it. Saying "I love you" is the open sesame to experience the Divine.

6. **Inspiration is more important than intention.**

    Intention is a toy of the mind; inspiration is a directive from the Divine. At some point you'll surrender and start listening, rather than begging and waiting. Intention is trying to control life based on the limited view of the ego; inspiration is receiving a message from the Divine and then acting on it. Intention works and brings results; inspiration works and brings miracles. Which do you prefer?

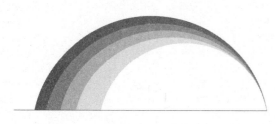

How to Heal Yourself (or Anyone Else) and Discover Health, Wealth, and Happiness

Here are two ho'oponopono proven ways to heal yourself (or anyone else) of anything you notice. Remember that what you see in another is also in you, so all healing is self-healing. No one else has to do these processes but you. The entire world is in your hands.

First, this is the prayer Morrnah said to help heal hundreds if not thousands of people. It's simple but powerful:

> Divine creator, father, mother, son as one . . . If I, my family, relatives, and ancestors have offended you, your family, relatives, and ancestors in thoughts, words, deeds, and actions from the beginning of our creation to the present, we ask your forgiveness. . . . Let this cleanse, purify, release, cut all the negative memories, blocks, energies, and vibrations, and transmute these unwanted energies to pure light. . . . And it is done.

Second, the way Dr. Hew Len likes to heal is to first say "I'm sorry" and "Please forgive me." You say this to acknowledge that something—without you knowing what it is—has gotten into your body/mind system. You have no idea how it got there. You don't need to know. If you are overweight, you simply caught the program that is making you that way. By saying "I'm sorry," you are telling the Divine that you want forgiveness inside yourself for whatever brought it to you. You're not asking the Divine to forgive you; you're asking the Divine to help you forgive *yourself*.

From there, you say "Thank you" and "I love you." When you say "Thank you," you are expressing gratitude. You are showing your faith that the issue will be resolved for the highest good of all concerned. The "I love you" transmutes the energy from stuck to flowing. It reconnects you to the Divine. Since the zero state is one of pure love and has zero limits, you are beginning to get to that state by expressing love.

What happens next is up to the Divine. You may be inspired to take action of some sort. Whatever it is, do it. If you aren't sure about the action to take, use this same healing method on your confusion. When you are clear, you'll know what to do.

This is a simplified version of the modernized ho'oponopono key methods of healing. To better understand the Self I-Dentity through Ho'oponopono process, sign up for a workshop. (See www.hooponopono.org.) To understand what Dr. Hew Len and I are doing together, see www.zerolimits.info.

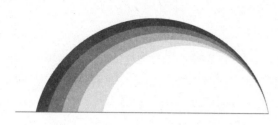

Who's in Charge?

Dr. Ihaleakala Hew Len

T hank you for coming along with me in reading this appendix. I am
grateful.

I love Self I-Dentity Ho'oponopono and dear Morrnah Nalamaku
Simeona, Kahuna Lapa'au, who so graciously shared it with me in November 1982.

This article is based on thoughts logged in my 2005 notebook.

9 January 2005

Problems can be solved **without knowing what the heck is going on!** Realizing and appreciating this is sheer relief and joy for me.

Problem solving, **part of the purpose for existence**, is what Self I-Dentity Ho'oponopono is about. To solve problems, two questions must be addressed: Who am I? Who's in charge?

To apprehend the nature of the cosmos begins with the insight of Socrates: "Know thyself."

21 January 2005

Who's in charge?

Most people, including those in the science community, deal with the world as being a physical entity. Current research in DNA to identify causes and remedies for heart disease, cancer, and diabetes is a prime example of this.

The Law of Cause and Effect: Physical Model

Cause	Effect
Faulty DNA	Heart Disease
Faulty DNA	Cancer
Faulty DNA	Diabetes
Physical	Physical Problems
Physical	Environmental Problems

The Intellect, the **Conscious Mind**, believes it is the problem solver, that it controls what happens and what is experienced.

In his book The User Illusion: Cutting Consciousness Down to Size, science journalist Tor Norretranders paints a different picture of Consciousness. He cites research studies, particularly those of Professor Benjamin Libet of the University of California at San Francisco, that show that decisions are made before Consciousness makes them, and that the Intellect is not aware of this, believing that it decides.

Norretranders also cites research that shows that the Intellect is only conscious of between 15 and 20 bits of information per second out of millions in reaction below its awareness!

If not the Intellect or Consciousness, then who's in charge?

8 February 2005

Memories replaying **dictate** what the Subconscious Mind experiences.

The Subconscious Mind experiences vicariously, **mimicking** and **echoing** memories replaying. It behaves, sees, feels, and decides exactly as memories **dictate**. The Conscious Mind too operates, without its awareness, by memories replaying. They dictate what it experiences, as research studies show.

The Law of Cause and Effect: Self I-Dentity Ho'oponopono

Cause	*Effect*
Memories Replaying in the Subconscious Mind	Physical—Heart Disease
Memories Replaying in the Subconscious Mind	Physical—Cancer
Memories Replaying in the Subconscious Mind	Physical—Diabetes
Memories Replaying in the Subconscious Mind	Physical Problems—the Body
Memories Replaying in the Subconscious Mind	Physical Problems—the World

The body and the world reside in the Subconscious Mind as creations of memories replaying, rarely as Inspirations.

23 February 2005
The Subconscious Mind and Conscious Mind, comprising the Soul, do not generate their own ideas, thoughts, feelings, and actions. As noted before, they experience vicariously, through memories replaying and Inspirations.

> But men may construe things after their fashion
> Clean from the purpose of the things themselves.
>
> William Shakespeare

It is essential to realize that the Soul does not generate experiences of its own, that it sees as memories see, feels as memories feel, behaves as memories behave, and decides as memories decide. Or, rarely, it sees, feels, behaves, and decides as Inspiration sees, feels, behaves, and decides!

It is crucial in problem solving to realize that the body and the world are not the problems in and of themselves but the effects, the consequences, of memories replaying in the Subconscious Mind! Who's in charge?

Poor soul, the center of my sinful earth,
[Thrall to] these rebel pow'rs that thee array,
Why dost thou pine within and suffer dearth,
Painting thy outward walls so costly gay?

William Shakespeare, Sonnet 146

12 March 2005

The **Void** is the **foundation** of Self I-Dentity, of Mind, of the cosmos. It is the **precursor state** to the infusion of Inspirations from Divine Intelligence into the Subconscious Mind. (See Figure C.1.)

All that scientists know is the cosmos was spawned from nothing, and will return to the nothing from whence it came. The universe begins and ends with zero.

Charles Seife, *Zero: The Biography of a Dangerous Idea*

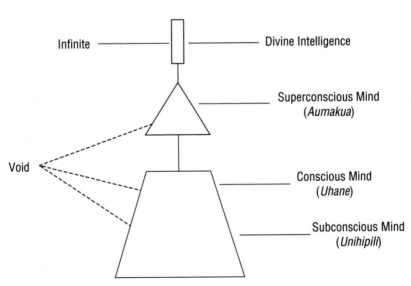

FIGURE C.1 State of Void

Memories replaying displace the Void of Self I-Dentity, precluding the manifestation of Inspirations. To remedy this displacement, to reestablish Self I-Dentity, memories need to be transformed to void through **transmutation** by Divine Intelligence.

> Clean, erase, erase and find your own Shangri-la. Where? Within yourself.
>
> Morrnah Nalamaku Simeona, Kahuna Lapa'au

> Nor stony tower, nor walls of beaten brass,
>
> Nor airless dungeon, nor strong links of iron,
>
> Can be retentive to the strength of spirit.
>
> William Shakespeare, Playwright

22 March 2005

Existence is a gift from Divine Intelligence. And the gift is given for the **sole purpose** of reestablishing Self I-Dentity through problem solving. **Self I-Dentity Ho'oponopono** is an updated version of an ancient Hawaiian problem solving process of **repentance, forgiveness,** and **transmutation.**

> Do not judge, and you will not be judged. Do not condemn, and you will not be condemned. Forgive and you will be forgiven.
>
> Jesus as reported in Luke: 6

Ho'oponopono involves the full participation of each of the four members of Self I-Dentity—Divine Intelligence, Superconscious Mind, Conscious Mind, and Subconscious Mind—working together as a unit of one. Each member has its unique part and function in problem solving memories replaying in the Subconscious Mind.

The **Superconscious Mind** is memory free, unaffected by memories replaying in the Subconscious Mind. It is always one with Divine Intelligence. However Divine Intelligence moves, so moves the Superconscious Mind.

Self I-Dentity **operates by Inspiration and memory**. Only one of them, either memory or Inspiration, can be in command of the Subconscious Mind at any given moment. The Soul of Self I-Dentity serves only one master at a time, usually memory the thorn instead of Inspiration the rose. (See Figure C.2.)

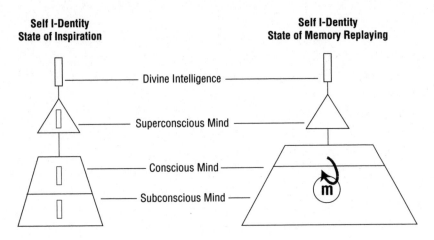

Self I-Dentity
State of Inspiration

Self I-Dentity
State of Memory Replaying

Divine Intelligence

Superconscious Mind

Conscious Mind

Subconscious Mind

FIGURE C.2   State of Inspiration and State of Memory Replaying

30 April 2005

> I am the self consumer of my woes.
>
> John Clare, poet

Void is the **common ground**, the equalizer, of all Self Identities, both "animate" and "inanimate." It is the indestructible and timeless foundation of the entire cosmos, seen and unseen.

> We hold these truths to be self-evident, that all men [*all life forms*] are created equal....
>
> Thomas Jefferson, U.S. Declaration of Independence

Memories replaying displace the common ground of Self I-Dentity, taking the Soul of Mind away from its natural position of Void and Infinite. Although memories displace the Void, they cannot destroy it. How can nothing be destroyed?

> A house divided against itself cannot stand.
>
> Abraham Lincoln

5 May 2005

For Self I-Dentity to be Self I-Dentity moment to moment requires **incessant Ho'oponopono**. Like memories, **incessant Ho'oponopono can never go on vacation. Incessant Ho'oponopono can never retire. Incessant Ho'oponopono can never sleep. Incessant Ho'oponopono can never stop as . . .**

> . . . in your days of gladness bear in mind
> the unknown evil [*memories replaying*] forging on behind!
> Geoffrey Chaucer, *Canterbury Tales*

12 May 2005

The Conscious Mind can initiate the Ho'oponopono process to release memories or it can engage them with blame and thinking. (See Figure C.3.)

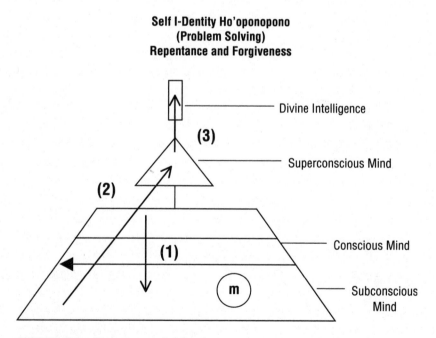

**Self I-Dentity Ho'oponopono
(Problem Solving)
Repentance and Forgiveness**

Divine Intelligence

(3)

Superconscious Mind

(2)

Conscious Mind

(1)

m

Subconscious Mind

FIGURE C.3   Repentance and Forgiveness

1. Conscious Mind initiates the Ho'oponopono problem solving process, a petition to Divine Intelligence to transmute memories to Void. It acknowledges that the problem is memories replaying in its Subconscious Mind, and that it is 100 percent responsible for them. The petition moves *down* from the Conscious Mind into the Subconscious Mind. (See Figure C.4.)

2. The down flow of the petition into the Subconscious Mind gently stirs memories for transmutation. The petition then moves up to the Superconscious Mind from the Subconscious Mind.

3. The Superconscious Mind reviews the petition, making changes as appropriate. Because it is always in tune with Divine Intelligence, it has the capacity to review and make changes. The petition is then sent up to Divine Intelligence for final review and consideration.

4. After reviewing the petition sent up by the Superconscious Mind, Divine Intelligence sends transmuting energy down into the Superconscious Mind.

5. Transmuting energy then flows from the Superconscious Mind down into the Conscious Mind.

6. And transmuting energy then flows down from the Conscious Mind into the Subconscious Mind. **The transmuting energy first neutralizes designated memories. The neutralized energies are then released into storage, leaving a Void.**

12 June 2005

Thinking and blame are memories replaying (see Figure C.2).

The Soul can be inspired by Divine Intelligence without knowing what the heck is going on. The only requirement for Inspiration, Divine creativity, is for Self I-Dentity to be Self I-Dentity. To be Self I-Dentity requires **incessant** cleansing of memories.

Memories are constant companions of the Subconscious Mind. They never leave the Subconscious Mind to go on vacation. They never

Self I-Dentity Ho'oponopono
(Problem Solving)
Transmutation by Divine Intelligence

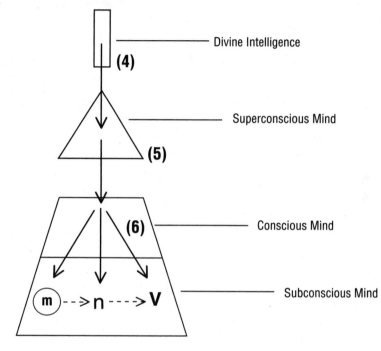

FIGURE C.4 Transmutation by Divine Intelligence

leave the Subconscious Mind to go into retirement. Memories never stop their incessant replaying!

The Man of Law's Tale

O sudden grief that ever art near neighbour
To worldly bliss! Sprinkled with bitterness
The ends of joy in all our earthly labour!
Grief occupies the goal to which we press.
For your own safety think it is no less,
And in your days of gladness bear in mind
The unknown evil forging on behind!

Geoffrey Chaucer, *Canterbury Tales*

To be done with memories once and for all, they must be cleansed to nothing once and for all.

It was in Iowa in 1971 that I fell head over heels in love for the second time. Dear M, our daughter, was born.

As I watched my wife care for M, I fell deeper and deeper in love with both of them. I had two wonderful people to love now.

After completing graduate school in Utah that summer, my wife and I had a choice to make: to go home to Hawaii or to continue graduate training in Iowa.

As we began life in the Hawkeye State, two hurdles immediately confronted us. First, M had never stopped crying after we brought her home from the hospital!

Second, the worst winter of the century in Iowa set in. Each morning for weeks on end I kicked the bottom inside of the front door of our apartment and hammered its edges with my hands to break the entombing ice on the other side.

Around her first year, bloodstains showed up on M's blankets. Only now as I write this sentence, I realize that the constant crying was her reaction to the severe skin problem that was diagnosed later.

I cried many a night as I helplessly watched M in fitful sleep scratching herself. Steroid medications proved powerless to help her.

By age three, blood seeped continuously from cracks in the crooks of M's elbows and knees. Blood wept from cracks around the joints of her fingers and toes. Thick mantles of hard skin covered the inside of her arms and around her neck.

One day nine years later, after we had returned to Hawaii, I was driving home with M and her sister. Suddenly, without conscious forethought, I found myself turning the car around and heading in the direction of my office in Waikiki.

"Oh, you folks have come to visit me," Morrnah said quietly as the three of us trooped into her office. As she shuffled papers on her desk, she looked up at M. "Did you want to ask me something?" she said softly.

M stretched out both arms, revealing years of pain and grief *etched in them up and down like Phoenician scrolls. "Okay," came Morrnah's reply, and she closed her eyes.*

What was Morrnah doing? The creator of Self I-Dentity Ho'oponopono was doing Self I-Dentity Ho'oponopono. A year later, 13 years of bleeding, scarring, pain, grief, and medications had come to an end.

Self I-Dentity Ho'oponopono student

30 June 2005

The purpose of life is to be Self I-Dentity as Divinity created Self I-Dentity in its exact likeness, Void and Infinite.

All life experiences are expressions of memories replaying and Inspirations. Depression, thinking, blame, poverty, hate, resentment, and grief are "fore-bemoanèd moans," as Shakespeare noted in one of his sonnets.

The Conscious Mind has a choice: It can initiate incessant cleansing or it can allow memories to replay problems incessantly.

12 December 2005

Consciousness working alone is ignorant of Divine Intelligence's most precious gift: Self I-Dentity. As such, it is ignorant of what a problem is. This ignorance results in ineffectual solving of the problem. Poor Soul is left to incessant, needless grief for its entire existence. How sad.

The Conscious Mind needs to be awakened to the gift of Self I-Dentity, "wealth beyond all understanding."

Self I-Dentity is indestructible and eternal, as is its Creator, Divine Intelligence. The consequence of ignorance is the false reality of senseless and relentless poverty, disease, and war and death generation after generation.

24 December 2005

The physical is the expression of memories and Inspirations taking place in the Soul of Self I-Dentity. Change the state of Self I-Dentity and the state of the physical world changes.

Who's in charge—inspirations or memories replaying? The choice is in the hands of the Conscious Mind.

7 February 2006 (A Leap into 2006)

Here are four Self I-Dentity Ho'oponopono problem solving processes that can be applied to reestablish Self I-Dentity through voiding memories replaying problems in the Subconscious Mind:

1. **"I love you."** When Soul experience memories replaying problems, say to them mentally or silently: "I love you, dear memories. I am grateful for the opportunity to free all of you and me." "I love you" can be repeated quietly again and again. Memories never go on vacation or retire unless you retire them. "I love you" can be used even if you are not conscious of problems. For example, it can be applied before engaging in any activity such as making or answering a telephone call or before getting into your car to go somewhere.

    > Love your enemies, do good to those who hate you.
    >
    > Jesus as reported in Luke: 6

2. **"Thank you."** This process can be used with or in place of "I love you." As with "I love you," it can be repeated mentally again and again.

3. **Blue solar water.** Drinking lots of water is a wonderful problem solving practice, particularly if it is blue solar water. Get a blue glass container with a nonmetallic cover. Pour tap water into the container. Place the blue glass container either in the sun or under an *incandescent* lamp (not a fluorescent lamp) for at least an hour. After the water is solarized, it can be used in several ways. Drink it. Cook with it. Rinse with it after a bath or shower. Fruits and vegetables love being washed in blue solar water! As with "I love you" and "Thank you" processes, blue solar water voids memories replaying problems in the Subconscious Mind. So, drink away!

4. **Strawberries and blueberries.** These fruits void memories. They can be eaten fresh or dried. They can be consumed as jams, jellies, and even syrup on ice cream!

27 December 2005 (A Leap Back into 2005)

I got the idea a few months back of a "talking" glossary of the essential "characters" in Self I-Dentity Ho'oponopono. You can get acquainted with each of them at your leisure.

Self I-Dentity: I am Self I-Dentity. I am composed of four elements: Divine Intelligence, Superconscious Mind, Conscious Mind, and Subconscious Mind. My foundation, Void and Infinite, is an exact replication of Divine Intelligence.

Divine Intelligence: I am Divine Intelligence. I am the Infinite. I create Self I-Dentities and Inspirations. I transmute memories to Void.

Superconscious Mind: I am Superconscious Mind. I oversee the Conscious and Subconscious Minds. I review and make appropriate changes in the Ho'oponopono petition to Divine Intelligence initiated by the Conscious Mind. I am unaffected by memories replaying in the Subconscious Mind. I am always one with Divine Creator.

Conscious Mind: I am Conscious Mind. I have the gift of choice. I can allow incessant memories to dictate experience for the Subconscious Mind and me or I can initiate the release of them through incessant Ho'oponopono. I can petition for directions from Divine Intelligence.

Subconscious Mind: I am Subconscious Mind. I am the storehouse for all of the accumulated memories from the beginning of creation. I am the place where experiences are experienced as memories replaying or as Inspirations. I am the place where the body and the world reside as memories replaying and as Inspirations. I am the place where problems live as memories reacting.

Void: I am Void. I am the foundation of Self I-Dentity and the Cosmos. I am where Inspirations spring forth from Divine Intelligence, the Infinite. Memories replaying in the Subconscious Mind displace me but do not destroy me, precluding the inflow of Inspirations from Divine Intelligence.

Infinite: I am Infinite, Divine Intelligence. Inspirations flow like fragile roses from me into the Void of Self I-Dentity, easily displaced by the thorns of memories.

Inspiration: I am Inspiration. I am a creation of the Infinite, of Divine Intelligence. I manifest from the Void into the Subconscious Mind. I am experienced as a brand-new occurrence.

Memory: I am memory. I am a record in the Subconscious Mind of a past experience. When triggered, I replay past experiences.

Problem: I am problem. I am a memory replaying a past experience again in the Subconscious Mind.

Experience: I am experience. I am the effect of memories replaying or Inspirations in the Subconscious Mind.

Operating System: I am the operating system. I operate Self I-Dentity with Void, Inspiration, and Memory.

Ho'oponopono: I am Ho'oponopono. I am an ancient Hawaiian problem solving process updated for today's use by Morrnah Nalamaku Simeona, Kahuna Lapa'au, recognized as a Living Treasure of Hawaii in 1983. I am composed of three elements: repentance, forgiveness, and transmutation. I am a petition initiated by the Conscious Mind to Divine Intelligence to void memories to reestablish Self I-Dentity. I begin in the Conscious Mind.

Repentance: I am repentance. I am the beginning of the Ho'oponopono process initiated by the Conscious Mind as a petition to Divine Intelligence to transmute memories to Void. With me, the Conscious Mind acknowledges its responsibility for the memories replaying problems in its Subconscious Mind, having created, accepted, and accumulated them.

Forgiveness: I am forgiveness. Along with Repentance, I am a petition from the Conscious Mind to Divine Creator to transform memories in the Subconscious Mind to Void. Not only is the Conscious Mind sorrowful, it is also asking Divine Intelligence for forgiveness.

Transmutation: I am transmutation. Divine Intelligence uses me to neutralize and to release memories to Void in the Subconscious Mind. I am available for use only by Divine Intelligence.

Wealth: I am wealth. I am Self I-Dentity.

Poverty: I am poverty. I am memories replacing. I displace Self I-Dentity, precluding the infusion of Inspirations from Divine Intelligence into the Subconscious Mind!

Before bringing this visit with you to an end, I would like to mention that reading this appendix satisfies the prerequisite of attending a Friday lecture if you are considering taking a Self I-Dentity Ho'oponopono weekend class.

I wish you peace beyond all understanding.

O Ka Maluhia no me oe.

Peace be with you,

Ihaleakala Hew Len, PhD

Chairman Emeritus

The Foundation of I, Inc. Freedom of the Cosmos

Bibliography

Bainbridge, John. *Huna Magic*. Los Angeles: Barnhart Press, 1988.

―――. *Huna Magic Plus*. Los Angeles: Barnhart Press, 1989.

Balsekar. *Consciousness Speaks*. Redondo Beach, CA: Advaita Press, 1993.

Berney, Charlotte. *Fundamentals of Hawaiian Mysticism*. Santa Cruz, CA: The Crossing Press, 2000.

Besant, Annie. *Thought Forms*. New York: Quest Books, 1969.

Blackmore, Susan. *Consciousness: An Introduction*. New York: Oxford University Press, 2004.

Brennert, Alan. *Moloka'i*. New York: St. Martin's Griffin reprint edition, 2004.

Bristol, Claude. *The Magic of Believing*. New York: Pocket Books, 1991.

Canfield, Jack, et al. *Chicken Soup from the Soul of Hawaii: Stories of Aloha to Create Paradise Wherever You Are*. Deerfield Beach, FL: Health Communications, 2003.

Carlson, Ken. *Star Mana*. Kilauea, HI: Starmen Press, 1997.

Claxton, Guy. *Hare Brain, Tortoise Mind: How Intelligence Increases When You Think Less*. New York: HarperCollins, 1997.

―――. *The Wayward Mind: An Intimate History of the Unconscious*. London: Abacus, 2005.

Dossey, Larry. *Healing Words: The Power of Prayer and the Practice of Medicine*. New York: HarperCollins, 1993.

Elbert, Samuel H. *Spoken Hawaiian*. Honolulu: University of Hawaii Press, 1970.

Ewing, Jim PathFinder. *Clearing: A Guide to Liberating Energies Trapped in Buildings and Lands*. Findhorn, Scotland: Findhorn Press, 2006.

Ford, Debbie. *The Dark Side of the Light Chasers*. New York: Riverhead Books, 1998.

Foundation of I, Inc. *Self I-Dentity through Ho'oponopono*. Honolulu, HI: Foundation of I, Inc., 1992.

Freke, Timothy. *Shamanic Wisdomkeepers: Shamanism in the Modern World*. New York: Sterling, 1999.

Glanz, Karen, Barbara K. Rimer, and Frances Marcus Lewis. *Health Behavior and Health Education: Theory, Research, and Practice*, 3rd edition. San Francisco: Jossey-Bass, 2002.

Haisch, Bernard. *The God Theory*. San Francisco: Weiser Books, 2006.

Hartong, Leo. *Awakening to the Dream: The Gift of Lucid Living*. Salisbury, UK: Non-Duality Press, 2001.

Horn, Mary Phyllis. *Soul Integration: A Shamanic Path to Freedom and Wholeness*. Pittsboro, NC: Living Light Publishers, 2000.

Husfelt, J. C., D.D. *The Return of the Feathered Serpent Shining Light of "First Knowledge": Survival and Renewal at the End of an Age, 2006–2012*. Bloomington, IN: AuthorHouse, 2006.

Irvine, William. *On Desire: Why We Want What We Want*. New York: Oxford University Press, 2006.

Ito, Karen Lee. *Lady Friends: Hawaiian Ways and the Ties That Define*. Ithaca, NY: Cornell University Press, 1999.

Kaehr, Shelley, and Raymond Moody. *Origins of Huna: Secret Behind the Secret Science*. Dallas, TX: Out of This World Publishing, 2006.

Katie, Byron. *All War Belongs on Paper*. Manhattan Beach, CA: Byron Katie, 2000.

―――. *Loving What Is*. New York: Harmony Books, 2002.

Katz, Mabel. *The Easiest Way*. Woodland Hills, CA: Your Business Press, 2004.

King, Serge Kahili. *Instant Healing: Mastering the Way of the Hawaiian Shaman Using Words, Images, Touch, and Energy*. n.p.: Renaissance Books, 2000.

Kupihea, Moke. *The Cry of the Huna: The Ancestral Voices of Hawaii*. Rochester, VT: Inner Traditions, 2005.

―――. *The Seven Dawns of the Aumakua: The Ancestral Spirit Tradition of Hawaii*. Rochester, VT: Inner Traditions, 2001.

Libet, Benjamin. *Mind Time: The Temporal Factor in Consciousness*. Cambridge, MA: Harvard University Press, 2004.

Libet, Benjamin, et al. *The Volitional Brain: Towards a Neuroscience of Free Will*. Exeter, UK: Imprint Academic, 2004.

Long, Max Freedom. *The Secret Science Behind Miracles: Unveiling the Huna Tradition of the Ancient Polynesians*. Camarillo, CA: DeVorss, 1948.

Macdonald, Arlyn. *Essential Huna: Discovering and Integrating Your Three Selves*. Montrose, CO: Infinity Publishing, 2003.

————. *Nurturing Our Inner Selves: A Huna Approach to Wellness*. Montrose, CO: Infinity Publishing, 2000.

McCall, Elizabeth. *The Tao of Horses: Exploring How Horses Guide Us on Our Spiritual Path*. Avon, MA: Adams, 2004.

Neville Goddard. *At Your Command*. Reprint edition. Garden City, NY: MorganJames Publishing, 2005.

Neville Goddard. *The Law and the Promise*. Camarillo, CA: DeVorss, 1984.

Noe, Alva. *Is the Visual World a Grand Illusion?* Charlottesville, VA: Imprint Academic, 2002.

Noland, Brother. *The Lessons of Aloha: Stories of the Human Spirit*. Honolulu, HI: Watermark Publishing, 2005.

Norretranders, Tor. *The User Illusion: Cutting Consciousness Down to Size*. New York: Penguin, 1998.

Patterson, Rosemary I. *Kuhina Nui*. n.p.: Pine Island Press, 1998.

Perkins, David N. *King Arthur's Round Table: How Collaborative Conversations Create Smart Organizations*. New York: John Wiley & Sons, 2002.

Polancy, Toni. *So You Want to Live in Hawaii*. Maui, HI: Barefoot Publishing, 2005.

Provenzano, Renata. *A Little Book of Aloha: Spirit of Healing*. Honolulu, HI: Mutual Publishing, 2003.

Ray, Sondra. *Pele's Wish: Secrets of the Hawaiian Masters and Eternal Life*. San Francisco: Inner Ocean Publishing, 2005.

Redfield, James. *The Celestine Prophecy*. New York: Warner Books, 1993.

Riklan, David. *101 Great Ways to Improve Your Life*. Marlboro, NJ: Self-Improvement Online, 2006.

Rodman, Julius Scammon. *The Kahuna Sorcerers of Hawaii*. Hicksville, NY: Exposition Press, 1979.

Rosenblatt, Paul C. *Metaphors of Family Systems Theory*. New York: Guilford Press, 1994.

Rule, Curby Hoikeamaka. *Creating Anahola: Huna Perspectives on a Sacred Landscape*. Coral Springs, FL: Llumina Press, 2005.

Saunders, Cat. *Dr. Cat's Helping Handbook: A Compassionate Guide for Being Human*. Seattle, WA: Heartwings Foundation, 2000.

Schwartz, Jeffrey. *The Mind and the Brain: Neuroplasticity and the Power of Mental Force*. New York: ReganBooks, 2002.

Seife, Charles. *Zero: The Biography of a Dangerous Idea*. New York: Penguin, 2000.

Shook, Victoria. *Current Use of a Hawaiian Problem Solving Practice—Ho'oponopono*. Sub-Regional Child Welfare Training Center, School of Social Work, University of Hawaii, Honolulu, 1981.

————. *Ho'oponopono: Contemporary Uses of a Hawaiian Problem Solving Process*. Honolulu: University of Hawaii Press, 1986.

Simeona, Morrnah N., et al. *I Am a Winner*. Los Angeles: David Rejl, 1984.

Steiger, Brad. *Kahuna Magic*. Atglen, PA: Whitford Press, 1971.

Vitale, Joe. *Adventures Within*. Bloomington, IN: AuthorHouse, 2003.

———. *The AMA Complete Guide to Small Business Advertising*. Lincolnwood, IL: NTC Business Books, 1995.

———. *The Attractor Factor: Five Easy Steps for Creating Wealth (or Anything Else) from the Inside Out*. Hoboken, NJ: John Wiley & Sons, 2005.

———. *Buying Trances: A New Psychology of Sales and Marketing*. Hoboken, NJ: John Wiley & Sons, 2007.

———. *Hypnotic Writing*. Hoboken, NJ: John Wiley & Sons, 2006.

———. *Life's Missing Instruction Manual: The Guidebook You Should Have Been Given at Birth*. Hoboken, NJ: John Wiley & Sons, 2006.

———. *The Seven Lost Secrets of Success*. Garden City, NY: MorganJames Publishing, 2005.

———. *There's a Customer Born Every Minute: P. T. Barnum's 10 Rings of Power for Fame, Fortune, and Building an Empire*. Hoboken, NJ: John Wiley & Sons, 2006.

———. *Turbocharge Your Writing*. Houston, TX: Awareness Publications, 1992.

———. *Zen and the Art of Writing*. Costa Mesa, CA: Westcliff, 1984.

Vitale, Joe, and Bill Hibbler. *Meet and Grow Rich*. Hoboken, NJ: John Wiley & Sons, 2006.

Vitale, Joe, and Jo Han Mok. *The E-Code*. Hoboken, NJ: John Wiley & Sons, 2005.

Wagner, David. *The Illusion of Conscious Will*. Cambridge, MA: MIT Press, 2002.

Wilson, Timothy. *Strangers to Ourselves: Discovering the Adaptive Unconscious*. London: Belknap Press, 2002.

Online Resources

www.attractanewcar.com

www.attractorfactor.com

www.BeyondManifestation.com

www.businessbyyou.com

www.clearingmats.com

www.cardiosecret.com

www.fit-a-rita.com

www.Healingpainting.com

www.hooponopono.org

www.JoeVitale.com

www.milagroresearchinstitute.com/iloveyou.htm

www.MiraclesCoaching.com

www.mrfire.com

www.SubliminalManifestation.com

www.thesecretofmoney.com

www.thesecret.tv

www.ZeroLimits.info

About the Authors

Dr. Joe Vitale is president of Hypnotic Marketing, Inc., an Internet marketing firm, and cofounder of Frontier Nutritional Research, a company specializing in proven anti-aging formulas. He's one of the stars of the hit movie, *The Secret*.

He is author of way too many books to list here, including the #1 best-selling books *The Attractor Factor: Five Easy Steps for Creating Wealth (or Anything Else) from the Inside Out* and *Life's Missing Instruction Manual: The Guidebook You Should Have Been Given at Birth*, and the best-selling Nightingale-Conant audio program, *The Power of Outrageous Marketing*.

His latest books include *Buying Trances: A New Psychology of Sales and Marketing*, *Hypnotic Writing*, *There's a Customer Born Every Minute*, *Meet and Grow Rich* (with Bill Hibbler), *The Greatest Money-Making Secret in History*, *Adventures Within*, *The Seven Lost Secrets of Success*, *The Successful Coach* (with Terri Levine and Larina Kase), and *The E-Code* (with Jo Han Mok). His next books will be *Your Internet Cash Machine* (with Jillian Coleman) and *The Key: The Missing Secret to Attracting Whatever You Want*.

You can sign up to receive Dr. Vitale's free monthly e-newsletter, "News You Can Use," at his main web site at www.mrfire.com.

Dr. Ihaleakala Hew Len has been involved in programs of problem solving and stress release for four decades. He spent three years as a consulting clinical psychologist at Hawaii State Hospital. He has worked with thousands of people over the years, including groups at the United Nations; UNESCO (United Nations Educational, Scientific, and Cultural Organization); International Human Unity Conference on World Peace; World Peace Conference; Traditional Indian Medicine Conference; Healers for Peace in Europe; and the Hawaii State Teachers Association.

He has been teaching the updated Ho'oponopono system worldwide since 1983. He co-presented the system at the United Nations three times with Kahuna Lapa'au Morrnah Nalamaku Simeona, designated a Living Treasure of Hawaii in 1983 for her creation of the updated Ho'oponopono. Dr. Hew Len applied the system successfully as staff psychologist from 1984 to 1987 in a high-security unit at the state psychiatric facility in Hawaii.

He has extensive experience working with developmentally disabled people and with the criminally mentally ill and their families. Today he travels and leads workshops on the Hawaiian method he loves, often with Dr. Joe Vitale.

His web sites are http://hooponopono.org/ and www.businessby you.com.

Index

How to Experience ZERO LIMITS Right Now

A Free Offer to Readers

Dr. Ihaleakala Hew Len and Dr. Joe Vitale have created a web site that "cleans" you as you view it. All you have to do is sit with it and allow the cleaning to take place. The site is at www.zerolimits.info.

If you are interested in the downloadable course on zero limits, which consists of audio CDs of a live presentation by the authors, and/or if you would like to experience a zero limits actual seminar with Dr. Hew Len and Dr. Vitale, simply go to www.zerolimits.info.

For a free Special Report on how to do Self I-Dentity Ho'oponopono to clear the blocks to health, wealth, and happiness, simply send a blank e-mail to zero@aweber.com.